Think Digital, Beyond Digital

Think Digital, Beyond Digital

How to Lead Inside by Stepping Outside

Rui Pedro Silva

BUSINESS EXPERT PRESS

Leader in applied, concise business books

Think Digital, Beyond Digital:
How to Lead Inside by Stepping Outside

Cover design by Anze Ban Virant—ABV atelier design

Interior design by S4Carlisle Publishing Services, Chennai, India

First published in 2026 by
Business Expert Press, LLC
222 East 46th Street, New York, NY 10017
www.businessexpertpress.com

ISBN-13: 978-1-63742-956-3 (paperback)
ISBN-13: 978-1-63742-957-0 (e-book)

Collaborative Intelligence Collection

First edition: 2026

10 9 8 7 6 5 4 3 2 1

EU SAFETY REPRESENTATIVE
Mare Nostrum Group B.V.
Doelen 72
4831 GR Breda
The Netherlands
gpsr@mare-nostrum.co.uk

Contents

List of Figures vii

Description ix

Preface xi

Part 1   **The Basis of a Transformation** 1

Chapter 1   The ASCEND Approach 3

Part 2   **Understand to Diagnose** 9

Chapter 2   The Understanding of Transformation 11

Chapter 3   The Understanding of Where You Stand 21

Chapter 4   The Understanding of Your Customers 61

Part 3   **How to Make the Right Decisions** 101

Chapter 5   Set the Foundations to Transform 107

Chapter 6   The Four-Floor Model 123

Chapter 7   The Disruption Through Technology 141

Part 4   **Building on Decisions and Make It Last** 187

Chapter 8   The SCRIPT Framework 189

Chapter 9   Behavioral Change 197

Chapter 10   Talent, Leadership, and Culture 207

Part 5   **Sustaining to Evolve** 213

Chapter 11   A Company's Readiness Through FRAME 215

Chapter 12   Beyond Digital, Toward What's Next 221

Bibliography 225

About the Author 229

Index 231

List of Figures

Figure 3.1 The digital transformation foundation.............................60
Figure 4.1 Success point. The intersection between customer,
problem, and value...76
Figure 6.1 The Four-Floor Model infographic...............................124
Figure 7.1 ASCEND Modeling Canvas 184

Description

Think Digital, Beyond Digital would change the way leaders think about and lead change. This book isn't about technology, it's about being clear, ready, and how people change. As "digital transformation" becomes a buzzword, Rui Pedro Silva gives us a grounded, evidence-based view based on both scientific research and his own experience as a leader in the real world.

Rui Pedro Silva has worked as an executive in many countries for more than 20 years and has published peer-reviewed research on how ready organizations are for change. He presents real-life cases with a practical and intellectually sound way to make changes. The book uses its own frameworks, such as ASCEND, FRAME, SCRIPT, ENRICH, Four-Floor Model and CORE5, to cover important aspects of change, such as strategic design, organizational readiness, cultural alignment, and behavioral evolution.

The ASCEND model is the main structure that guides the book. It takes readers through six pillars of change: Acceptance, Self-Reflection, Customers and Market, Strategy, Planning and Execution, and Change and People. This helps leaders link abstract strategy with real action. We look at each phase through real-life examples, reflective questions, and structured tools that make change both measurable and human.

The FRAME model, validated by academics, is a way to find out how ready an organization really is to change. It looks at five important areas: Formula (Business Model), Relevant (Market), Alignment (Strategy), Muscle (Organization), and Engine (Processes). This gives leaders a way to figure out what's wrong before they do anything.

The SCRIPT framework (Scope, Capital and Capabilities, Roadmap, Implementation, Progress, and Tracking) gives you a structured way to turn strategy into results from start to finish. It turns transformation into a structured, repeatable process that leaders can control and measure.

Rui Pedro Silva, on the other hand, says that change doesn't last just because of the process, it lasts because of the people. The ENRICH model

(Engage, Reflect, Intent, Change) explains how people go from being aware of something to changing their behavior. These frameworks, along with CORE5 (Role Modeling, Personality, Perception, Context, Individuality), connect systems and culture, design and behavior.

Silva questions common ideas about management throughout the book. He replaces jargon with clear language, templates with thought, and copying with purpose. He says that change isn't about doing what others do; it's about asking the right questions in the right order and having the courage to see the organization as it really is.

Think Digital, Beyond Digital is both a guide and a way to think about things. It is for business leaders, consultants, and academics who want to connect vision and action, culture and ability. It's for people who think that the future of leadership isn't about knowing all the answers but about learning how to think through change.

Preface

We live in fascinating times. Technology is no longer just something that supports our businesses; it has become the very heartbeat of how we work, compete, and connect with the world. Digital transformation has become one of those phrases everyone throws around, but behind the buzz lies a very real challenge: How do we actually make it work? How do we take an organization—large or small, traditional or modern, public or private—and truly reimagine it for the digital age?

That is the journey of this book.

I'm Rui Pedro Silva, and I've spent my career inside boardrooms and on the ground floors of global companies, leading transformations that at times felt exhilarating—and at other times felt like steering a ship through a storm. What I've learned—sometimes the hard way—is that success in digital transformation doesn't come from chasing every shiny new app or drowning teams in more technology. It comes from clarity. From people. From strategy. From understanding what truly creates value for customers and aligning the entire organization to deliver on that promise.

This book is not a dry manual, nor is it a lofty piece of theory. It is a guide built from real-life lessons, practical tools, and yes—a few scars from transformations that didn't go as planned. You'll find models that simplify complexity, stories that bring ideas to life, and a step-by-step journey that takes you from defining why transformation matters to actually making it happen in practice.

Along the way, we'll travel together through stories that mirror the reality of businesses everywhere. We'll stop in Porto to visit Mrs. Sarah, who ran a small clothing shop until a pandemic closed her doors—and discovered how digital commerce and logistics-as-a-service could turn her local boutique into a business with global reach. We'll step into a tiny Portuguese shoe store that could only ever sell to the handful of people walking down its street—until digital opened the doors to millions of potential buyers. We'll look at Netflix buying a Spanish TV series that barely made a dent at home but exploded into a global cultural phenomenon once given the right platform: *La Casa de Papel*. We'll compare Booking.com's rise with the traditional travel agency and ask how legacy companies can reinvent themselves before disruption sweeps the floor out from under them.

These aren't just anecdotes. They're signposts of the broader truth: Digital transformation isn't about technology for its own sake—it's about rethinking value, scale, and the role people play in shaping the future.

We'll talk about customers—because transformation needs customers at its core. We will talk about people, because no technology will take over the need to have talented people, to have strong leadership, to have a winning culture. We will look deep into strategies, models, decisions that can make the difference. We won't forget the execution, however, as that's the place where dreams fail or succeed. My promise to you as a reader is simple: You won't just understand digital transformation better. You'll be able to see it, feel it, and know how to act on it. Whether you are a CEO trying to reimagine a legacy organization, a manager tasked with leading change, or simply a curious professional preparing for the future, this book is designed to give you both perspective and practical ways forward.

Above all, I want to demystify digital transformation. It isn't magic. It isn't reserved for Silicon Valley giants. It is a process of asking the right questions, making the right choices, and creating the right conditions for people and technology to work together. And yes—it can even be fun, once you cut through the noise and focus on what really matters.

Technology has been around for a long time and has changed how we live, work, and connect. But in the past 10 years, its presence has changed completely. Technology is no longer just a background tool; it is now the basis for how economies work, how businesses compete, and how people see the world.

Let's look at the Brand Finance report from 2020, for instance. Companies like Amazon, Google, Apple, Microsoft, Meta, Samsung, Huawei, and WeChat were the most valuable brands in the world. Seven of the top 10 were basically tech companies. In 2000, only 20 years ago, Coca-Cola, Marlboro, McDonald's, and Ford were some of the most valuable brands in the world. At that time, only Microsoft, IBM, Intel, and Nokia could be called "real" tech companies. In other words, technology went from being 40 percent of the top global brands to 70 percent in just 20 years. That is not just a trend; it is a revolution.

This revolution has changed whole industries. With the iPhone, Apple changed the way people think about mobile phones. It changed not only telecommunications but also music, photography, and even payments. Amazon changed the way people buy and sell things all over the world, not just in the United States. Netflix changed the way we think about entertainment in a big way. Disney+, which is a streaming service, helped Disney stay ahead of Netflix and Amazon in the streaming wars. Disney used to be a big name in films and theme parks.

These big companies aren't the only ones who will be affected. Every business, from a two-person start-up to a century-old multinational, has to rethink how it works, how it gets customers, and how it stays competitive because of their success. People expect the same level of speed, personalization, and convenience from their bank, insurance company, or even the small store on the corner after getting used to Amazon or Netflix.

And that leads us to the main questions I've heard over and over again in my career:

- Why is there so much talk about digital transformation but so little understanding of it?
- Why do some businesses do well on this journey while others do not?
- Why do younger people seem to adapt to this digital world so easily, while older organizations often have trouble?

These are not just ideas. CEOs in boardrooms, managers in workshops, entrepreneurs over coffee, and students in classrooms all ask these kinds of questions. They show a common struggle: knowing that digital transformation is no longer an option but not knowing how to make it work.

Why This Book and Why Now

In my professional journey, I've seen too many leaders overwhelmed by the term "digital transformation." For some, it feels like a trendy buzzword thrown around in conferences. For others, it represents something dangerously abstract: a costly initiative with no guaranteed outcome. Many mix up digital transformation for simply "implementing technology"—buying a new system, setting up an e-commerce site, or creating a social media presence. But transformation is not about installing technology. It is about rethinking how a company creates, delivers, and captures value in a digital-first world. And it is confusing because there is no single recipe for digital transformation. What works for a Silicon Valley start-up may not work for a Portuguese family-owned retailer. What drives success in a global logistics giant may not translate to a regional health care provider. Yet, across industries and geographies, I've found that the principles of transformation—the ways to *think* about digital—remain surprisingly consistent.

This book is my attempt to share those principles. It is not a manual of tools and apps; it is a practical guide to *thinking digital, beyond digital*—a way to deconstruct the myth of transformation and provide you with frameworks, questions, and stories that simplify complexity without underestimating it.

The timing could not be more urgent. The COVID-19 pandemic accelerated digital adoption by what some estimate to be a decade. Companies that were hesitant about online sales, remote work, or cloud-based services suddenly had no choice. Consumers who never ordered groceries online started doing so weekly. Entire industries—from education to health care—were forced to adopt digital practices almost overnight. And while the pandemic may be behind us, the acceleration it triggered is irreversible.

The only real question is no longer "if" or "when" to transform. It is only "how."

What Is My Story

However, before we dive deeper, I want to share a little bit of my story, as that story is central to why this topic matter so much to me.

Do you know Fão? I guess not. Fão is the best place in the world but only known by a few. A small town in the municipality of Esposende, in Portugal. It doesn't have more than 3,000 inhabitants. I was born there, almost four decades ago. Let's just say, it wasn't exactly a hub of innovation. My parents were hardworking people, earning modest salaries.

Technology was not a part of my childhood—not because I lacked interest but because we lacked the means.

Instead, my childhood was defined by simple joys: a ball, a dirt pitch, two improvised goals, and the feeling that every neighborhood game was a European final. There were no smartphones, no social media, no streaming services. Still, we had all we needed.

The luxury of growing up in that beautiful place by the coast in the north of Portugal taught me two important things:

- Resilience: I saw people struggling just around the corner. I saw families working day in and day out to be able to make ends meet.
- Fragility: I saw how dependent entire communities were on small businesses—supermarkets, factories, local shops—that could collapse overnight if a big company would open up in the region or if production was moved abroad. These experiences shaped my conviction that competitiveness is not just about size. It is about adaptability, talent, and the ability to use whatever tools are available—today, that tool is digital.

Ironically, my journey into technology happened almost by accident. I studied engineering for a while but never finished. And yet, I entered the tech field with curiosity and hunger. Without a degree, I built a career not through credentials but by creating value—solving problems with technology in ways that mattered to people.

Over the years, that curiosity led me from technical roles into leadership positions. I've had the privilege of serving in senior executive roles in global companies like A.P. Moller-Maersk and Adidas. In 2020, I was honored to be named Best Digital Leader in Europe by CIONET. This recognition was not simply about my own work but about the collective wisdom I absorbed from peers across industries—from leaders at Shell, Heineken, Coca-Cola, Nike, KLM, and beyond. And despite this global experience, I often think back to Fão. To the fragility of local businesses. To the realization that digital transformation, if understood and used wisely, can be a great equalizer. It can allow a small clothing store in Porto to sell internationally. It can give a start-up in Lisbon access to the same cloud infrastructure as a multinational. It can provide opportunities to talent in Indonesia or Poland or Brazil to contribute to global projects without ever leaving their town.

That is why I wrote this book: to share what I've learned, not only for large corporations but for any organization, any leader, any person who wants to understand and act on the possibilities of digital.

What Is at Stake

Digital transformation is no longer just about tech. In a world where customers can choose from an infinite number of options and reach people all over the world, it's about staying alive, being relevant, and growing.

These stories are not made up. You will meet Mrs. Sarah, a shopkeeper in Porto who learns about the benefits of e-commerce and international logistics as a service. You will learn how a small-town shoe store can stay hidden or grow into a global business if it goes digital. You will learn about Fresh Paintings, a company that changed the way it does business by bringing together internal and external talent on a digital platform.

These are not stories from fairy tales. They are real-life situations that many businesses deal with every day. Some people succeed by changing, while others fail by not changing. It's not usually the technology itself that makes a difference. The difference is having a vision, being a good leader, and being able to think in digital terms.

This is where the paradox lies. The speed of technological change has sped up—artificial intelligence (AI), cloud, blockchain, IoT—but the success rate of digital transformations has stayed low. A lot of research says that 60 to 70 percent of changes don't give the value they were meant to. Why? This is because businesses care more about technology than people. Because they mix up strategy with activity. Because they don't think culture, communication, and alignment are important enough.

This book says that change isn't something you do once and then stop. You "become" it. When you learn a new language, there is a time when you are always translating in your head. But at some point, you become fluent. That fluency is "Thinking Digital," where digital isn't just a project but the way things are done.

What You Can Expect from This Book

I want to give you more than just buzzwords. I want to help you understand and feel confident, and provide you with useful tips on how to make digital transformation real.

- You will learn how to look at your business and the market.
- You will learn how to make plans that link vision to action.
- You will learn how digital twins and other methods can change business models.
- You will learn how to plan execution, measure success, and make changes as you go.
- You will see why people—skills, behavior, and leadership—are always the focus.

This book is for CEOs of big companies, small business owners, team leaders, students getting ready to lead in the future, and anyone who wants to know more about what digital transformation really means. The rules apply no matter how big or small your business is, from a restaurant with 10 employees to a company with a thousand.

This book's main goal is to make the knowledge of digital transformation available to everyone. Making it easy to find, understand, and use for everyone, since digital is everywhere these days.

So, let's get started. Together, we will think digital, beyond digital.

PART 1

The Basis of a Transformation

Introducing the ASCEND way of thinking

If there's one thing I've learned after years of working in digital transformation, it's this: Change does not fail because of bad PowerPoints or poor technology. It fails because organizations rush into action without truly understanding themselves, their customers, or the people who will have to live with the change.

I've seen companies pour millions into technology programs, only to realize that nobody wanted what they built. I've also seen small family businesses succeed where giants failed—simply because they asked the right questions before moving.

That's why I built the approach ASCEND, standing for Acceptance, Self-Reflection, Customers and Market, Execution and Strategy, Navigation and Planning, Drive People and Change.

ASCEND is not a rigid approach or a sequence. It is a guide for thinking, a conversation that leaders can have with themselves, their teams, and their organizations. It breaks down the complexity of transformation into six natural pillars, each grounded in questions rather than prescriptions.

The name is intentional. Transformation is not about quick wins or shortcuts. It's a climb. A step-by-step journey that requires preparation, endurance, and belief in the destination. ASCEND provides the footholds:

- **A**cceptance
- **S**elf-Reflection
- **C**ustomers and Market

- **E**xecution and Strategy
- **N**avigation and Planning
- **D**rive People and Change

If you will read this book chapter by chapter, you'll notice something: Each of these letters mirrors the structure of the book itself. Every major chapter corresponds to a step in this ascent.

Together, they form a guiding approach—from recognizing reality to embedding change in people.

There are two aspects that are worth pointing to begin with:

- One aspect you will see, is that in times I will refer as the transformation being centered around customers, or the transformations starting with the customer, on the other hand in ASCEND, you see it as the third letter. Both are true. Consider the *A* and *S*, often times as the prework, the needed education to embrace in change. Some will ask, could I do *C* before *S*, and the answer is yes. You will see that there is no strict sequencing that one must follow 100 percent. It is a guidance of thinking, rather than a prescription.
- Drive People and Change shows up as the last step. Once again, I refer back the principle of a model to guide thinking, not necessarily something you can't address differently. People and Change are not a sequential step of a process. Those are almost overarching across the whole journey, and you will see in that chapter, there it is no strict dependency from *N*.

CHAPTER 1

The ASCEND Approach

Transformation can be overwhelming if we try to eat it whole. ASCEND breaks it into digestible pillars. Think of it less as a project plan and more as a set of powerful conversations. Because when leaders pause to ask the right questions, clarity emerges, alignment forms, and the climb becomes possible. Conversations can happen back and forth, and that's the principle of this approach.

Acceptance

Transformation begins when we stop pretending everything is fine.

For many leaders, this is the hardest step. It requires looking at uncomfortable truths: falling revenues, new competitors, shrinking relevance. Without this moment of honesty, all the strategies in the world are just theater.

I've met CEOs who still insisted, even in 2020, that their customers "would never buy online." Months later, COVID closed their shops, and reality arrived. Acceptance came late —and cost them dearly.

Contrast that with companies that recognized the signs early. Retailers who saw the rise of Amazon didn't wait for a pandemic to invest in e-commerce. They accepted change before it was forced on them.

Acceptance is not panic. It's urgency without hysteria. It's saying:

- Why do we need to change now?
- What happens if we don't?
- What is truly at stake?

This is the foundation. Without acceptance, people don't mobilize. With it, momentum builds naturally.

Self-Reflection

After you realize that you need to change, an important piece of the journey happens when look in the mirror.

Organizations often get "mirror blindness," which means they only see what they want to see and not what's really there. Leaders think that digital maturity is higher than it is, that cultural resistance is lower than it is, or that weak processes don't matter because they're too close to them.

Self-reflection means asking hard but important questions, like: What are our real strengths?

- Where do we need to get stronger?
- Are all our teams really ready for change?
- Where do we belong?
- How are we perceived outside by our customers?

I used to work for a manufacturing company that spent a lot of money on robots. It looked like a leader in automation from the outside. But when we talked to the workers, we found that there were big silos, bad collaboration, and not much digital literacy. The machines were new, but the culture was stuck in the past. People, not technology, were the real problem for them.

Confidence is based on clarity. It stops leaders from building castles on sand.

Customers and Market

If there's a golden rule in transformation, it's this: If you're not serving the customer, you're just adding complexity.

Many companies transform inward—new systems, new processes—but forget to look outward. Yet customers are the reason transformation exists. Their needs, habits, and frustrations are the compass.

Consider Mrs. Sarah, a shop owner from Porto we will meet later. For years she relied on local foot traffic. When the pandemic shut her doors, she discovered that her customers wanted the convenience of online shopping. By listening outward—through digital platforms, through feedback—she opened a new channel and found growth.

The questions here are actually rather quite simple:

- What do customers truly value?
- How are their behaviors shifting?
- What are competitors doing that we are not?

Looking outward lets us think forward. It reminds us that transformation is not about shiny tech but about people who buy, choose, and remain loyal.

Execution and Strategy

Now we move from "why" and "what" into "how."

Strategy is often misunderstood. Too many leaders think it's a 50-page document with lofty visions. In reality, strategy is about clarity and choices. I like to say,

Strategy it is lot more about what not to do, than what to.

What will we do? What will we not do? Where will we focus?

I like to connect this phase to the Four-Floor Model we will introduce later in detail:

- Define a clear strategic statement (what success looks like).
- Set success criteria (how we'll measure it).
- Identify the problems preventing success.
- Design solutions that solve those problems.

Take the case of Fresh Paintings, the wall-art company, that we will know in detail later in the book. Their strategic statement was simple: "We want every customer to personalize their home with affordable, artistic wall paintings." From there, they defined criteria (booking times, satisfaction scores), problems (lack of visibility, limited artist supply), and solutions (a digital platform connecting internal and external painters).

Strategy provided the compass; execution gave them the legs to walk.

The questions here:

- What are our transformation goals?
- How do we align leadership and teams?
- How do we measure success, so it's not just talk?

Without clarity, execution drifts. With it, strategy fuels momentum.

Navigation and Planning

Without a plan, a strategy is just a dream. Navigation turns desire into organized movement.

This is where you decide what your top priorities are, what resources to use, and what milestones to reach. It's also where governance comes into play.

Companies try to "do everything at once" too often. This leads to teams that are all over the place, wasted energy, and no clear progress. To navigate means to break the mountain into smaller climbs.

One company I worked with wanted to make a digital twin of their business. They didn't try to do everything at once. Instead, they started small by going after low-margin customer groups with a simpler digital model. After it worked, they expanded into bigger markets. They built up their confidence little by little.

The questions to ask are:

- What do we need to do now?
- How do we make the best use of our resources?
- What are the most important points and milestones we need to reach?

Navigation makes sure that we don't just dream about change; we make it happen.

Drive People and Change

Lastly, the most important part of change, though not the last but rather overarching: people.

People decide if technology works, even if it causes change. There are two parts to this phase:

1. Change Management—setting up the framework: communication plans, ways to give feedback, risk logs, and metrics for how well things are going.
2. People and Leadership—making people want to do things, not just telling them what to do. In this case, we will talk about a few models that become useful tools for employees to understand why change is important, think about their role, build intention, and change their behavior, with leaders showing them how to do each step.

I remember, in a company I met some years ago, when a sales team was told to "sell digitally" overnight. At first, they said no. There were rewards for making sales, but the tools were hard to use, and no one explained why. When leaders changed incentives, put money into digital training, and made things clear, adoption went through the roof. It wasn't the technology that made the difference; it was the people.

The questions that drive us are:

- How do we create intention instead of forcing instruction?
- How can we give leaders the power to lead the way?
- How do we not only track activity but also changes in behavior?

This is where transformation goes from being a project to being part of the culture.

How ASCEND Shapes This Book

ASCEND is more than six pillars. It's a philosophy: pause, ask, reflect, align, and only then move.

Too many transformations fail not because leaders lacked ambition but because they skipped these conversations. They chased speed instead of clarity. They acted before aligning.

With ASCEND, we take the time to breathe before we sprint. We accept reality. We reflect inward. We look outward. We craft strategy. We navigate with discipline. And above all, we drive people, because change without people is just an illusion.

Transformation is not a straight line. You may loop back, revisit questions, or repeat pillars. That's not failure—that's learning. The climb is iterative.

The question isn't whether your company will face digital change. It already is. The question is how you'll face it—with confusion or with clarity, with fear or with courage.

ASCEND gives you the footholds. The climb is yours to make.

By introducing the concept of the six pillars of ASCEND, I present the guiding structure of this book. Throughout the following chapters, we will revisit each of these pillars, equipping you with the tools and knowledge to lead the essential conversations across them.

The remainder of this book is divided into six parts:

- **Part 2—Understand to Diagnose**
  How organizations must accept the need for change, reflect on their own journeys, and diagnose their current state in relation to their markets and customers.
- **Part 3—How to Make the Right Decisions**
  How to evolve from diagnosis to a concrete set of choices and actions that drive meaningful transformation.
- **Part 4—Building on Decisions and Make It Last**
  How to move from decision to execution, creating the structures and processes needed to ensure initiatives are delivered effectively, and embed the right behaviors so that transformation endures and becomes part of how the organization operates.
- **Part 5—Sustaining to Evolve**
  How to bring all the pieces together, maintaining focus and energy over time to ensure continuous adaptation and growth.

Every meaningful transformation starts with a mirror. Before deciding what to do, leaders must have the courage to see their organization as it truly is—its strengths, its blind spots, and its capacity to change. That reflection marks the beginning of the journey ahead, explored in the next part of this book.

PART 2

Understand to Diagnose

Understanding Where You Stand and Whom You Serve

Every change starts with understanding what needs to change, why it needs to change, and what is stopping it from happening. That clarity begins with acceptance: being willing to see things as they are without any filters or excuses. Organizations often rush to come up with new plans or start digital projects without really knowing where they are right now. But you can't start a journey without a clear starting point.

Two important moments: Acceptance and Reflection. It requires leaders to examine the organization's strengths, weaknesses, and the assumptions that inform its decisions. It means checking to see if the current business model still works in the market, if the culture is open to change, and if the company's "engine" is ready to run at the speed that change needs. SWOT (strengths, weaknesses, opportunities, and threats), readiness assessments, and capability mapping are not just pieces of paper; they are mirrors that show how ready the company is for what is coming.

But thinking about things must also go outward. Knowing the company is just as important as knowing the market and the customer. Who are we helping? What problems are we really fixing? How are people's hopes changing? The answers to these questions determine not only relevance but also survival.

This section looks at that double reflection, both inside and outside. It starts with acceptance, which means realizing that change starts with accepting the truth. Then comes self-reflection, where leaders look at their organization's strengths, weaknesses, and connections to their customers and markets. These chapters set the stage for everything that comes next: decisions that are made with care, actions that are based on a goal, and change that lasts.

CHAPTER 2

The Understanding of Transformation

A couple of years ago, back in my home country, a famous Portuguese textile company went bankrupt. The reasons for the collapse are not public, but it is not the first in the industry and probably won't be the last. Every time I read a story like this, it makes me think about how far along small- and medium-sized businesses are in their digital transformation and how hard it is for many leaders to really understand what it means to digitalize a business.

These kinds of bankruptcies all raise the same basic question: Could the business keep up with changes in the market? Too often, the answer is no. The situation may be different, but the pattern is the same. Many businesses are going under not because the market has left them but because they didn't realize how deep and urgent the changes needed to be.

Acceptance is the first phase in the ASCEND approach for this reason. Leaders must first face the facts before they can make a plan, use technology, or carry out their plans. They must realize that the market has changed, the rules of competition have changed, and what worked yesterday may not work tomorrow. No change can happen without acceptance.

Practical Case: Our Clothes

Our Clothes was a Portuguese textile company that started in 1940. It became a must-have in city centers because of its classic style, and by the mid-1990s, it had 30 stores across the country.

The company had made the equivalent of €4 million in sales by 1995. As department stores and malls became more popular, Our Clothes changed by opening new stores in these modern places. Sales went up three times between 1995 and 2017. The brand was in every major mall, and it looked like it would keep growing.

Management was sure of its position and held on to a simple idea: Good clothes bring people into the store. People didn't care as much about technology, marketing innovation, and digital skills. Systems stayed old, and not much money was put into updating them.

2020 came next.

The pandemic closed all stores that weren't necessary. Overnight, sales in stores dropped to zero. There was a lot of inventory. The money stopped coming in. Competitors, on the other hand, both big chains and nimble start-ups, boosted their online sales through e-commerce platforms and marketplaces. Customers who had to shop online quickly learned how easy and fast it was, as well as new rules about returns and shipping.

In May 2020, Our Clothes held an emergency board meeting to talk about selling things online. There was a split in the leadership team. Some people said that the brand's loyal customers would never leave the store. Others said that the company's future was in danger if it didn't start doing business online. Months went by. The debts kept piling up.

The business finally decided to put money into online sales by November 2020. But at that point, it was too late. The technology was old, the employees didn't know how to use it, the marketing wasn't very good, and there wasn't much of a presence on social media. The effort felt like it was thrown together and desperate because there wasn't much money.

Sales were still slow four months later. Even worse, the company was now losing customers to smaller competitors that had adopted e-commerce earlier and offered easy online shopping, reliable delivery, and simple returns.

In May 2021, only 18 months after the pandemic started, Our Clothes went bankrupt because it couldn't pay its suppliers and workers. In less than two years, a brand that had been around for 80 years had gone out of business.

Reflection

The end of Our Clothes is not just a story about a disease. It's a story about not being able to accept change. Long before COVID-19, there were signs of digital disruption, but management held on to the idea that their old formula—selling quality clothes in physical stores—was enough.

It was too late by the time they realized they needed to go digital.

This is why Acceptance is the right there in the very early pillar of ASCEND. No business can really change if it doesn't accept that the market is changing, technology is changing, and customer expectations are changing.

The story of Our Clothes is made up, but it is a lot like what many businesses went through during the pandemic. A lot of people found out too late that a strong position in today's market can fall apart almost overnight if you don't keep investing in technology and digital readiness. If you don't pay attention to this, you could lose customers—both consumers and business clients—to competitors who are more flexible.

It's important to remember that digital transformation is not the same as putting in place a new ERP (enterprise resource planning) system or making an iPhone app. Technology is a part of the journey, but change is much bigger. It's about changing the way the company works, how it makes money, how it interacts with customers, and how it organizes itself to compete in a world where digital is the first choice.

We will look at two important points in the rest of this chapter:

- What digital transformation really means—going beyond buzzwords to define it as a full process, not just an upgrade to the technology.
- Who should and shouldn't go digital? This means looking into when digital transformation is needed and when it might not be.

These points of view will help you understand why Acceptance is such an important phase on any journey of change.

The Meaning of Digitalizing a Company

To digitalize a company is not about doing digital things—it is about becoming digital at the core.

It's funny that the form has changed more than the content in the digital age. The goals of business are still the same: get customers, sell things, build loyalty, and make money. What has changed is how to reach those goals.

Yes, we live in a time when technology is changing in ways that have never happened before, and new business models are being created. Every day, new businesses start up. But digital transformation isn't just about getting new technology for the sake of it. It's about getting rid of limits. A lot more is possible now than it was 15 years ago, and customers expect those things to be real.

Practical Case: Selling Cars

Think about what it's like to buy a car. Sixteen years ago, the best thing you could do was make an appointment at a dealership, go to the showroom, and talk to a salesperson. You can now buy a car completely online.

Platforms like bynco.com show what it really means to go digital. Bynco is more than just a place to buy used cars. It combines many services into one smooth experience:

1. Quality of certified vehicles
2. Service checks and maintenance
3. Pickups and deliveries of trade-ins at your door
4. A 14-day free return policy

Bynco has basically made it as easy to buy a car as it is to buy a pair of shoes online. Instead of copying the traditional dealership model, they came up with a new way to make the customer experience better by fixing real problems:

1. Buying a car takes a lot of time and is annoying.
2. A short test drive doesn't show you everything.
3. Buyers are worried about problems that aren't obvious and a lack of openness.

Bynco built trust, convenience, and uniqueness by using technology to fix these problems. That's the best kind of digitalization: technology that helps the customer, not technology for technology's sake.

What Is Digital Transformation?

Digital transformation is when you look at a business from the inside out and outside in and come up with a plan to help it reach its goals. This plan should include using technology to make the business run better, interact with customers better, and find new ways to grow and compete.

It's not about making an app or putting in an ERP system. It means thinking about the whole value chain from the customer back and then figuring out which technologies will help you reach that goal.

Not Perfection, but Adaptation

Charles Darwin famously said, "It is not the strongest and smartest species that survives. It is the one that can change the most easily."

The same idea applies to digital transformation. It doesn't matter if your product is the best if customers don't want it anymore or if they can get it faster, easier, or cheaper somewhere else. The fall of Our Clothes, which was talked about earlier, is a perfect example of this: They had quality and tradition, but they couldn't change.

A lot of businesses still have trouble changing. Some common reasons are:—unclear visions,—wrong technology choices,—weak organizational structures, or—not knowing what role digital should play in their strategy.

All of these failures are due to the same mistake: starting with technology instead of the customer.

Starting with the customer is the only way to make digital transformation work. What do they want? What issues are they trying to fix? What do they expect now based on their experiences in other fields?

A business can only then design processes, choose technologies, and build services that really help. The rest is just details.

Who Should or Shouldn't Digitalize

The short answer is everyone.
Digital transformation affects all industries, all types of businesses, and all parts of the world. There is no doubt about it; the only question is how and when.

Digitalization Is Not Optional

This is an uncomfortable truth for some leaders. They think that "big tech" companies like Uber, Amazon, or Airbnb are the only ones that can go through digital transformation. Or they think it only applies to big companies with thousands of employees and budgets in the billions of euros. That is not true at all.

Digitalization is now a basic requirement for staying competitive. Customers want digital convenience no matter what they're buying, whether it's shoes from a corner store or a global logistics service. Digital processes are becoming more and more important to suppliers, regulators, and employees as well. Not paying attention to this is not a plan; it's a countdown to being irrelevant.

The Principle Doesn't Change, but the Scale Does

It's clear that a business with three employees can't change in the same way as one with three thousand. The level of complexity changes. But the logic doesn't.

1. For a small bakery, going digital could mean allowing customers to order and have their food delivered through a local app.
2. For a textile maker, this could mean making their production tracking and supply chain systems digital.
3. For a global retailer, this could mean rethinking the whole customer journey across dozens of markets and channels.

The principle is the same in all cases: use technology to do things better, help customers more, and get ready for the future.

Timing Matters

If digital transformation is going to happen no matter what, the real question is when. Like Our Clothes earlier, waiting too long to act can lead to failure. If you act too soon without self-reflecting, and the customer needs, you could waste resources. Leaders must be able to tell when the market is changing and get ready before it happens.

A New Level of Competition

The truth is that digitalization has changed what it means to be competitive. What used to be "nice to have" is now just expected:

1. Customers want online and offline experiences to be the same.
2. Workers expect digital tools to help them do their jobs.
3. Partners want systems that work together.

Not providing this baseline is no longer an option; it is simply falling behind.

Practical Case: The Restaurant of Mr. Francis

Mr. Francis has been running a small restaurant on a quiet street next to St. John's Hospital in Porto for more than 25 years. His specialty is the *francesinha*, a dish that people loved so much that they would go out of their way to find his secret spot.

Business was good for a long time. Customers came in droves, and Mr. Francis didn't have to worry about anything but the kitchen. People still did their accounting on paper. For him, technology didn't matter. Why bother when people kept coming back for the same meal they loved?

Then 2020 came.

The pandemic made him close his business. When he opened again, he noticed something troubling: Fewer customers were coming back. Sales kept going down over the course of several months. The situation was very bad by 2021.

On a rainy April afternoon, Mr. Francis sat in his empty restaurant and looked at the tables where his regular customers used to sit. He asked himself:

"Why? It doesn't make any sense. The quality of the *francesinha* is still the same."

He was right: The quality hadn't changed. The customer had changed. People were spending less time around the hospital. A lot of people wanted delivery. Some people found new restaurants online. Competitors quickly added ordering apps, delivery partnerships, and social media presence.

Mr. Francis was only interested in the product. But in the digital age, quality is only one part of the puzzle. Accessibility, visibility, and ease of use are all equally important.

Reflection

Mr. Francis's story isn't about food; it's about how to adapt. A great product could be hard to find if it isn't easy to see and use online. His *francesinha* was still good, but it wasn't as useful in a market that had changed.

Going digital doesn't mean giving up on tradition. It's about making sure that tradition is still available in a world where customers want to find, order, and use products in new ways.

Two Faces of Digitalization: Beyond Mr. Francis

A lot of people learned during the pandemic that ordering food delivered to their home has its benefits. They could get good food without having to leave the couch. This is a big change in what we now think of as a basic service. It doesn't mean that all restaurants will be empty, but it does explain why Mr. Francis's is.

Customers loved his *francesinha* so much that they were willing to go through the trouble of going to his restaurant before the pandemic. The trade-off changed after 2020. Distance was no longer a problem thanks to platforms like Uber Eats or Glovo. His dish was no longer just competing with restaurants in Porto's city center. It was also competing with Mr. Charles, Mr. Thiago, and dozens of other people who were delivering *francesinhas* without even needing a restaurant.

There was no digitalization of the food itself. It was the service model. Convenience, visibility, and accessibility became the most important factors. Some went even further and used Instagram or TikTok campaigns to send people to their delivery channels. Ordering a *francesinha* online became as easy and common as ordering pizza for a lot of people.

But not every industry works like restaurants do. Think of little stores that sell trinkets. In this case, the business model is based on people buying things on a whim. People go in for a pen and leave with five things they didn't expect. How does digitalization work here?

The answer is not the same. Digitalization in these stores doesn't always mean making an app for delivery. Instead, it can mean using data to keep track of sales, figure out which products sell best, look at how sales change with the seasons, and run small tests with window displays or campaigns. A store can learn which products to stock, which to promote, and which to stop selling with even the simplest tools. This will help the store lose less money and make more money.

This gives us two important views on digitalization:

1. External perspective: changing the way we serve and reach customers (e.g., restaurants that used to only serve food now deliver it)
2. From the inside: We want to make our operations and decision making better (e.g., stores use sales data to improve their inventory).

The best changes use both. Businesses need to find a balance between innovating for customers and doing a great job with their own operations. You have to do both.

We will later see how these points of view fit into the key combination of our key five pillars of digital transformation success: Market, Business Models, Strategy, Organization, and Processes, together with the four building blocks of transformation: External Positioning, Products, Technology, and Operations.

CHAPTER 3

The Understanding of Where You Stand

One of the most frequent questions I hear from leaders is: "Where do we even begin with digital transformation?"

The truth is that the starting point is rarely obvious. Some companies start with technology, buying new systems in the hope that digitalization will somehow follow. Others start with marketing, rushing to create an app or social media presence. And many start with cost cutting, assuming that efficiency is the same as transformation.

All of these approaches risk missing the essence. Digital transformation does not start with technology. It is centered around the customers, and it needs a proper prework: clarity of self. Without a clear vision of *why* you are transforming and *what problem you are solving*, any investment becomes guesswork.

Think of it like building a house. You wouldn't begin by buying bricks and cement before knowing the kind of home you want. You'd start with a blueprint: what is this house for, who will live in it, what lifestyle will it support? Only then would you decide on the materials, the contractors, the layout.

The same logic applies to digital transformation. The real starting point is not the tool, the platform, or the app. The center point is the customer. Who are they? What do they expect? What are their frustrations today? And how will we solve those frustrations in a way that creates new value for both sides? This center point requires some self-understanding to build that centeredness.

This is why many companies stumble. They confuse action with direction. Buying a new ERP is action. Launching an app is action. But without direction, these actions risk being scattered and ineffective.

Getting started means not rushing to do everything at once but focusing on the *right* key steps. Small wins create momentum, and momentum builds transformation.

Before we prescribe, we need a clear starting point. This chapter focuses on the discipline of seeing the organization as it truly is—its strengths, constraints, and readiness for change—so decisions rest on evidence, not assumptions.

Looking in the Mirror

While a transformation should always center around the customer, you can't succeed in transforming without doing a self-reflection. Before looking at markets, technologies, or competitors, you need to look inward and understand your company's current position. One of the most effective—and accessible—tools for doing this is the SWOT analysis.

What does SWOT stand for:

- Strengths—What are we good at? What do customers already value in us?
- Weaknesses—Where are we falling short? What slows us down?
- Opportunities—Which trends, technologies, or shifts in the market could we take advantage of?
- Threats—What risks or external pressures could put us at risk?

At first glance, SWOT may seem simplistic. In reality, when used with discipline, it is one of the best ways to open an honest conversation about the company's reality. It forces leaders to articulate, in concrete terms, what they believe defines the organization today.

Take note: A good SWOT is not a brainstorming exercise where every idea goes on the board. It is a prioritization exercise. A company might have dozens of strengths, but usually only two or three truly define its competitive edge. The same goes for weaknesses: Identifying the most critical gaps is what makes this tool useful.

A SWOT is not about producing a pretty slide; it's about clarity. And clarity is what allows leaders to move to the next stage with a shared understanding of where the company stands.

The main objectives of a SWOT analysis are:

- To synthesize the internal and external analysis that must be carried out on the company.
- Identify where the main areas of focus should be.
- Identify the main risks for the company.
- Helping to understand the areas in which greater investment should be made (Strengths). The areas in which there should be greater commitment in order to create a positive impact (Opportunities). The areas that matter most because they affect what is positive (Weaknesses) and the main risks to the company's success (Threats).

In practical terms, Strengths and Weaknesses refer to the company's internal environment, that is, identifying what the company is very good at or not.

On the other hand, Opportunities and Threats refer to the external environment, because they clearly define the areas for investment to improve the company's position or to prevent it from being more exposed to being overtaken by the competition.

Although not a completely simple process, it is a very important one because it will help to better understand the company's current situation.

Let's go back to Mr. Francis and his restaurant to understand the application of SWOT:

Let's imagine a scenario in which Mr. Francis didn't let the restaurant fail due to lack of demand. Somewhere in the middle of 2020, he realized something was changing. He didn't know where to start, but he invested time in a SWOT analysis.

Here's the simplified result:

Strengths:
- The quality of the *francesinha*
- A secret family recipe
- Strong reputation
- Loyal customer base built over many years

Weaknesses:

- Overreliance on one signature dish
- No innovation of new dishes in recent years
- Restaurant location hard to access without a car
- Limited parking
- No delivery service

Opportunities:

- Customers frequently ask for delivery
- Growing demand for *francesinhas* via home delivery platforms
- Ability to join Glovo, Uber Eats, and so on with minimal investment
- Potential to create new dishes or sauces based on the secret recipe

Threats:

- Rising competition from restaurants offering delivery
- *Francesinha* is a common regional dish, so copycats are easy
- Delivery speed gives competitors in better locations an edge

From this simple analysis, seven conclusions emerge:

1. Reputation is a strength → Invest in it.
2. Product is strong → Keep quality high.
3. Delivery is missing → Fix it fast.
4. Limited menu → Expand strategically.
5. Market clearly wants home delivery.
6. Market also wants variations on the famous sauce.
7. Competitors are already moving faster.

Seven points. Simple, practical, and actionable.

Notice something important: In Francis's case, the emphasis falls naturally on business model and market. In another business, it might be different. But whatever the focus, the real value of SWOT is not the four lists themselves—it's the ability to structure insights into decisions.

The Questions That Matter

A SWOT exercise is only as good as the questions you ask. Here are four you can always consider:

- What kind of company am I?
  Not in terms of size, but in profile. Am I a specialist? A generalist? A cost leader? Strengths and weaknesses often come straight from this profile.
- What market do I belong to?
  A company only exists if there's a market. Understanding that market is essential to identifying opportunities and threats. You may wonder if we talk about market in self-reflection, then why do we have Customers and Market later? It is a very good question and just highlights what I mentioned before. It is about a process of questioning, analyzing. Some themes happen across many pillars, while its depth may differ.
- What is my company's positioning?
  Even in a small town, why do customers choose one café over another? Answering this reveals where your real threats and opportunities lie.
- Which digital transformation should I follow?
  Transformation is not about adopting tech blindly. It's about designing what the company should *be*—and defining what role technology plays in achieving that. Once again, this question could eventually trigger some thoughts in terms of solutions and strategy. It does. It triggers questions and points that will need more detail later.

Why This Matters

Think of a navigation system. If you don't define your current location, it can't tell you how to reach your destination. The same is true for digital transformation: If you don't know where you stand, you can't chart the path forward.

Unlike GPS, it's not impossible to find a way without defining your starting point.

But it will be slower, more painful, and far more expensive.

The Formula, Relevance, Alignment, Muscle, Engine

Once reflection provides clarity, structure must follow. The FRAME model translates awareness into analysis—helping you assess readiness across business model, market, strategy, organization, and processes. It turns reflection into an actionable diagnosis.

While there are no magic formulas for defining a company profile, understanding the fundamentals is a key step in any strategy. Companies differ in size, complexity, and industry, but all can be understood through a set of core pillars that determine how they operate and how they grow.

From an internal point of view, this analysis becomes more complex as organizations scale. Yet, the same foundations apply whether we are talking about a three-person start-up or a multinational with thousands of employees.

In my experience, every company rests on five main pillars, what I call FRAME:

- Formula (Business Model): what business models the company supports or intends to support, and their ability to comprehend them and pivot
- Relevance (Market): the market it operates in, its positioning or ambition within that market, and the clarity of its value proposition
- Alignment (Strategy): how its business strategy is understood (sometimes even more than defined), both overall and across areas like HR, finance, or commercial
- Muscle (Organization): how the company is structured and managed operationally and commercially
- Engine (Processes): the processes that ensure customers are served

These five pillars (FRAME) form the basis of a company's identity, and they define the likelihood of the transformation's success. When they are managed well, the company moves closer to success. When they are weak or misaligned, digital transformation becomes fragile. FRAME is a lot more about what behaviors the company shall display to maximize the results of a transformation, than the actual transformation itself.

If you wonder why these five, and what is the logic behind each of those in much more detail, the scientific process to conclude is documented in the research carried out by Silva et al.[1]

It is important to note that there is no strict order for working on these pillars. Some are naturally interdependent—for example, you cannot design a new business model without a supporting strategy, nor set a strategy without understanding the market. But taken together, they provide a complete map of where a company is and how prepared it is for digital transformation.

Successful businesses can have excellent processes, talented people, and cutting-edge technology—but unless these are integrated into a coherent formula, relevance, alignment, muscle, and engine, their transformation efforts remain fragmented.

Ultimately, the five pillars help leaders distinguish between internal focus (processes and organization), external focus (market and business models), and the bridge between them: strategy. They not only describe the DNA of a company but also reveal its maturity for digital success.

To make this concrete, let's briefly look at each of the five pillars. Each one highlights a different dimension of how a company operates, and together they form the foundation on which any digital transformation strategy must be built.

Formula: Business Model

The research carried out by Silva et al.[2] indicates that business model refers to "All aspects relate to how the company operates, the products it offers, and how it innovates within those areas."

---

[1] Rui Pedro Silva, Henrique São Mamede, and Vitor Santos, "Clarification of the Present Understanding of the Assessment of an Organization's Digital Readiness in SMEs," *Emerging Science Journal* 7, no. 6 (2023): 2279–307.

[2] Rui Pedro Silva, Henrique São Mamede, and Vitor Santos, "A New Proposed Model to Assess the Digital Organizational Readiness to Maximize the Results of the Digital Transformation in SMEs," *Journal of Innovation & Knowledge* 10, no. 1 (2025): 100644.

Most of the time, businesses make a business model and stick with it for years. They don't want to change it because they don't want to be seen as failing. Changing a business model is not a sign of failure; it's a sign of strength. Look at Netflix as an example. It started out as a DVD rental service, but it changed into the streaming service we know today, with amazing results.

It's not easy to change a business model, especially for companies that have been around for a long time. It means rethinking the people, processes, and even the organization itself. But it's often necessary. For example, Volvo started a car subscription service where customers pay a monthly fee that covers the car and all of its maintenance. You can cancel this subscription every three months, unlike a regular lease or purchase. This model speaks directly to a new generation of buyers who care more about access and flexibility than ownership.

These kinds of changes go against decades of tradition. For most of modern history, "buying a car" meant having a contract, credit, and ownership. People can now treat a car like a Spotify account. Other markets are also changing because of similar disruptions. For example, meal delivery services and shared mobility services like electric scooters are changing what convenience means.

In the end, digitalization isn't just adding new technology to the old way of doing things. It's about asking yourself if your current business model still works in the market you want to be in and if your products still solve the real problems your customers have.

Relevance: Market

The research carried out by Silva et al.[3] indicates that market "focuses on all aspects of the company's market approach, its customers, and its value proposition."

No matter its size, every company must deeply understand the market it operates in. Without this, it's impossible to define the value customers expect or to position products in a way that truly resonates. Ultimately, it is not the company that defines the market—it's the customers.

---

[3]Silva et al., "A New Proposed Model to Assess the Digital Organizational Readiness to Maximize the Results of the Digital Transformation in SMEs," 100644.

Too often, companies analyze the market only through the lens of past experience. This backward-looking perspective is especially dangerous for large organizations, where stability and tradition can blind them to new realities. Start-ups, meanwhile, are born with an eye on emerging trends and can disrupt entire industries in a fraction of the time.

Understanding the market means more than knowing your current customers—it means anticipating where they are going. If demand shifts toward delivery platforms like Uber Eats, then building a sophisticated ordering system on your restaurant's own website may add little value. Likewise, in hospitality, most hotels have direct booking engines, but many prioritize platforms such as Booking.com because that's where entire segments of customers actually make their decisions.

In short: Analyzing the market is about knowing who your customers are, where they are, and what they value today and tomorrow. This understanding becomes the compass for how technology should be applied and where investments should be made.

Alignment: Strategy

The research carried out by Silva et al.[4] indicates that strategy "focuses on various aspects of the organization's strategic setting, from strategic planning to change management or technology."

Strategy is the road map that shows us how to get there if the market indicates the way. It serves as the binding agent that binds the company's business model, market, organization, and procedures together to form a cohesive whole. Even the best products or the most cutting-edge technologies run the risk of becoming dispersed initiatives with minimal long-term impact if they lack a strategy.

Defining a strategy is about making decisions, not just announcing lofty objectives. Clear answers to the following basic questions are necessary for strategy:

- Which goods or services should be our top priorities?
- Which clients are we interested in serving, and which are not?

---

[4]Ibid.

- Which channels of distribution work best for our market?
- How are we going to position ourselves in relation to our competitors?
- Which pricing strategy best captures the realities of the market and value creation?

Consider a business that sees a definite shift in the market toward online shopping. Knowing that the trend exists is not enough. Deliberately planning which products to sell online, how to market them, which logistics partners to collaborate with, and how to provide a unique customer experience are all essential to success. Without this, the business runs the risk of blindly copying rivals and entering the digital sphere without making an impression.

Additionally, a strong strategy compels organizationwide alignment. The financial strategy must guarantee that resources are allocated to the appropriate priorities, the HR strategy must support the skills required for the transformation, and the commercial strategy must directly relate to the purchasing habits of customers. This connectivity guarantees that the business operates as a cohesive system rather than in pieces.

Lastly, strategy is dynamic. Similar to how a GPS recalculates when the road changes, it must adapt to the market. A strategy that worked five years ago may become obsolete today if it ignores new technologies, customer expectations, or competitive threats. The companies that thrive are those that treat strategy as a living process—always grounded in purpose, but flexible in execution.

Muscle: Organization

The research carried out by Silva et al.[5] indicates that organization "focuses on foundational organizational aspects such as a company's structure, people, or culture."

When people hear the word "organization," they frequently picture intricate charts, levels of management, or bureaucratic procedures. The reality is that an organization is just the way a business organizes and

---

[5]Ibid.

mobilizes its people, partners, systems, and structures in order to produce value and accomplish goals. It is the operating muscle that makes the company run smoothly, not just the number of workers or the boxes on an organogram.

Consider Partying, a small business that hosts events and birthday celebrations in retirement communities. On the surface, it appears to be composed of just three performers. However, the picture is more comprehensive because the external accountant who guarantees tax compliance and the outsourced social media service that attracts new clients are also components of the organizational system. Since the service could not be successfully provided without each component, they come together to form the actual organization.

An important point is demonstrated by this example: An organization is not just its internal employees. It comprises every supplier, partner, and service provider that adds to the value chain of the business. A reductionist perspective that runs the risk of underestimating the organization's actual scope is to think of it as just "our employees."

One of the most important factors in digital transformation is organization. People and their organizational structure are what change a company, not technology alone. Even with significant investments in state-of-the-art systems, an organization that is poorly organized—with disjointed teams, remote decision making, or leaders who are not tech-savvy—will find it difficult to transform. On the other hand, a well-organized organization that has distinct roles, open lines of communication, and the capacity to work with outside partners fosters an environment that is conducive to the efficient use of technology.

Organization also refers to capability and culture. It determines how fast decisions are made, how adaptable teams are to changing circumstances, and how well staff members (and partners) comprehend the possibilities of digital tools. Rigid hierarchies and siloed functions are frequently obstacles in a digital age where speed and customer proximity are crucial. Cross-functional, agile structures with open communication are more likely to be successful.

In the end, the organization is the company's main strength since it carries out the plan, makes the processes possible, and links the business model to the marketplace. Digital transformation initiatives run the risk of being like a brilliant plan on paper with no one to execute it if the organization is not ready for change.

Engine: Processes

The research carried out by Silva et al.[6] indicates that processes "focus on how the company manages its processes and generally governs its working methods."

Processes are perhaps the most straightforward of the five pillars to explain, yet they are often the hardest to sustain over time. A process is simply the sequence of steps through which a company delivers value— whether to customers, employees, or partners. It could be taking an order, manufacturing a product, onboarding a new employee, or resolving a customer complaint. In other words, processes are the *engine* that keeps the company moving.

While the concept is simple, the challenge comes in maintaining efficiency and relevance as the company grows. Processes tend to multiply and become more complex in proportion to the size and diversity of the organization. What worked when a company had 10 employees often becomes a bottleneck when it has one hundred. The difference between a thriving company and one that stagnates often lies in whether it can continually redesign its processes to adapt to new demands.

Well-designed processes are crucial in digital transformation because they are the areas where technology can create the most visible impact. Automating invoicing, digitalizing inventory management, or implementing a CRM (Customer Relationship Management) system to track customers are all examples of how processes can be redesigned to become faster, cheaper, and more accurate. But digitalization is not about simply taking an old manual process and moving it online—it is about asking whether the process is still necessary, how it can be simplified, or even whether it should exist at all.

The key is to identify which processes are *critical*. For a technology services company, project quality assurance might be essential; for a

---

[6] Ibid.

computer retailer, the repair and return process may be the differentiator. Knowing what the few truly essential processes are allows leaders to focus resources on improving them continuously. The clearer these processes are, the easier it is for the organization to scale, adapt, and serve customers effectively.

Another essential point is that processes exist for one purpose only: to enable the company to deliver value to its customers (and employees) with quality and efficiency. Any process that does not contribute to this goal is, at best, administrative noise—and at worst, a distraction that drains energy from the organization. Digital transformation offers an opportunity to look at every process with a fresh perspective: Does it add value, can it be simplified, can it be automated, or can it be eliminated?

In this sense, processes are not just about efficiency. They are about alignment—ensuring that every step in the company's operations is working toward the same promise of value to customers. A well-designed process can turn strategy into execution; a poorly designed one can prevent even the best strategy from being realized.

High-Level View of the Market

With the internal view established, we now turn outward. Understanding market shape, forces, and trajectory completes the diagnostic baseline that will guide choices later on.

You can't change something if you don't know what it is. If you don't know the market you work in and the customers who shape it, any effort to go digital will fail. No change without customers.

A market is not a label; it's a way of looking at things. It depends on the business model, the product, the location, the channel, and even the rules. For practical reasons, think of your market as the group of people who have a problem that your current (or easily changed) product can solve. In other words, don't start with the category you think you're in; start with the problem you can solve.

Keep in mind, however, in this phase the level of detail is not the same as you will have in the next chapter. In this phase, it is about market size, who is part of that market, overall addressable market, and so on.

Practical Case 1: The Shoe Shop of Mrs. Joanne and Mr. Edward

For more than 20 years, Mrs. Joanne and Mr. Edward have been running a store where they make shoes by hand. Their shoes are known for being high quality, which makes the store one of the most important places to buy things in their small town in the Vila Real area.

The store is in a small neighborhood with about 2,000 people, but the town has about 15,000 people. It is thought that about 50 percent of the 2,000 people who live there could be interested in buying shoes. That makes the shop's immediate market 1,000 people.

The shop does sometimes get customers from other towns, but not very many because it doesn't spend much on advertising outside the city. This extra volume is thought to be between 20 and 50 people. Mrs. Joanne and Mr. Edward have a market of about 1,050 people who could buy from them.

The store sold shoes to 100 different people in 2024. This is about 10 to 12 percent of the people who could be customers. In short, the store currently has 100 customers, but if it fully tapped into its local market, it could grow to 1,050.

Case 1: Final Thoughts

This example assumes that digital commerce does not affect the market. We can break the shoe store's situation down into three levels of market potential, representing it in very simple terms.

- The whole market is the 2,000 people who live nearby.
- Addressable Market: After using criteria like age, consumption habits, or gender, the number of potential buyers drops to 1,000 of the 2,000 inhabitants and extends with additional 50 from additional towns.
- Conquered Market: 100 customers, or about 10 percent of the potential

This simple breakdown shows how important it is to understand the market: It helps the business figure out its real growth margin and what part of the demand is still unmet.

The market could be worth about €168,000 a year if each of the 1,050 potential buyers bought three to four pairs of shoes at an average price of €40. The store is only able to get about €16,000 right now, which is only 10 percent of that amount.

The real value of this analysis is in what comes next: figuring out why. Why do 100 people buy here and 950 do not? What do these 950 people look for in shoes that makes them go to other stores? No matter how big or small the company is, every leader should be asking these kinds of questions.

Only some of the people who come into the store buy something. If 300 people came in 2024 and only 100 bought something, that means one out of three people becomes a customer and two out of three leave. Getting some of this "lost" 66 percent could have as big of an effect as getting new customers.

An important in making things happen is to "write them down" or better saying keeping track of why people don't buy—through a few direct questions, this data makes it easier to make better decisions. If customers are hesitant to buy shoes because there isn't a comfortable place to try them on, that information points directly to a change that could boost sales.

This case is about a small family business, but the same logic works for medium and large businesses as well. The difference is in size: Their possible markets must be bigger, but the idea stays the same. To be successful, you need to know everything about the customers you already serve and the ones you haven't reached yet.

Practical Case 2: Repair Services

Repair Services has 150 workers and makes €4 million a year. It installs, fixes, and checks water heaters, central heating systems, and solar panels.

There are 150 people who work for the company, and 135 of them are technical experts. The other 15 work in the office and administration.

When you look at the money:

- Each technician makes about €30,000 in sales every year.
- Each technician costs about €27,000 a year (salary and other costs).
- This means that each technician contributes €3,000.

The total contribution is about €405,000 when you multiply that by the 135 technicians. This money has to pay for the salaries of the 15 office workers and all other business costs.

The company's books look like this:

Sales	€4,050,000
Technical costs	€3,645,000
Gross margin	€405,000
Office staff costs	€405,000
Other costs	€250,000
Final result	(−€250,000)

Even though the business seems to have a lot of customers, it loses €250,000 a year.

When we look more closely, we see that each technician does about 300 repairs a year, and each one costs about €100. This comes out to about 1.3 repairs per day per technician over the course of 225 working days. But since a typical repair takes two hours and an hour of travel, each technician can actually do 2.6 repairs a day.

This means that the business is only using about half of its technical capacity.

The implications are striking: The company could theoretically double its output without hiring more workers, just by making sure that technicians are as productive as possible and that there is enough demand. This is what the financial model for such a situation would look like:

Sales	€8,100,000
Technical costs	€3,645,000
Gross margin	€4,455,000

Office staff costs	€405,000
Other costs	€500,000
Final result	(+€3,550,000)

From a €250,000 annual loss to more than €3 million in profit—purely by tapping into the unrealized potential of the existing workforce.

Case 2: Final Thoughts

This example illustrates a crucial point: While the customer centricity is just core, it is just fundamental to have this prework done properly. Especially in a running business, look at capacity and how is that capacity maximized today. At times, that will make more results than a massive, large transformation. Funny enough, in many moments … the little things are the ones that make the biggest difference.

Repair Services is not failing because of a lack of talent or resources. In this case, we could even argue, it is not failing because of customers or what they sell. On the contrary, it has 135 technicians operating at just 50 percent of their capacity. In purely operational terms, the company has enough people to double its output without adding headcount, as long there is demand for more work. The challenge lies in either:

1. Market activation: generating enough demand to match the available supply
2. Make the best of the capacity in place: Is it working at half capacity due to lacking demand, or due to poor planning?

If we assume the first option, at first, the simple conclusion could be to cut the workforce in half, balancing costs with the current level of demand. While this might solve the immediate financial problem, it would also reduce the company's ability to scale and capture growth in the future. Cost cutting is often the easiest path, but rarely the most sustainable one.

The more strategic alternative is to focus on growth rather than reduction. By identifying where new customers are, what services they need, and how to reach them more effectively, Repair Services could increase its sales volume significantly without any increase in staff. This approach would not only restore profitability but also create the conditions for sustained expansion.

If the company manages to fully utilize its technicians' potential, the numbers are impressive: It could move from a €250,000 annual loss to more than €3 million in annual profit, purely by aligning its market presence with its operational capacity.

The key insight here is that companies are not blank slates when starting a transformation journey. They bring with them an existing set of assets, processes, and untapped potential. Understanding the true state of the company—its strengths, limitations, and especially its hidden capacity—is fundamental. Only then can digital transformation be used not just to solve immediate inefficiencies but to unlock new levels of performance and growth.

Both cases highlight the same underlying truth: Understanding the market dynamics is not optional—it is the foundation of any transformation.

In the case of Mrs. Joanne and Mr. Edward's shoe shop, the challenge lies in recognizing the difference between the *total market*, the *addressable market*, and the *conquered market*. Their real opportunity is not only in serving the 100 loyal customers who already buy from them but in identifying the 950 who could be buying but are not—and uncovering why. Without this understanding, growth is left to chance.

In the case of Repair Services, the issue is not demanding visibility but capacity utilization. With 135 technicians working at only 50 percent of their potential, the company carries a structural imbalance: enough resources to double its service output, but insufficient sales to match. Here, the opportunity is not about cutting costs but about aligning market strategy with operational capability, turning losses into profits through smarter customer acquisition and market activation.

Together, these cases show that markets must be understood from two sides:

- On the *demand side*, knowing the customers who buy, the ones who don't, and why
- On the *supply side*, knowing the company's true capacity and potential, and how much more of the market it could serve if demand were unlocked

This kind of approach is very important if you want to truly maximize the results of a digital transformation. Without understanding the market, the company serves and the potential for maximizing existing resources, it will be much more difficult to succeed in a transformation.

However, as we've touched on a little in this chapter, it's not enough to know the market's potential. You need to identify how you can gain market share (or protect what you already have). This is a prerequisite for identifying the best approach to digital transformation. Winning market share (or protecting it) is intrinsically linked to a company's right to win market share. The right, in this case, means having better products, being more competitive, having the right price, and so on. Identifying this right involves defining the company's positioning in each market.

That's exactly what we'll cover in the next chapter.

Company's Positioning

In any market, it's not size that earns you the right to win—it's the strength of your solution and the value it brings. The companies that rise are the ones solving real problems, not just taking up space.

As we discussed in the previous chapter, the right to stand out in a given market is defined by the quality of what you offer and how competitive you are. It is therefore crucial for companies to frequently ask themselves: *What is my right to win?* Put differently, what makes customers choose our company over others—and keep choosing it?

Take a small café in a quiet European town. What is its right to attract more customers than the café next door? Is it the taste of the espresso? Is that alone enough to sustain loyalty? Sometimes yes, often no.

When Sport TV appeared in Portugal, it created a new differentiator. Many cafés began installing the service on their televisions, transforming themselves into weekend gathering spots where people could watch football together. This wasn't just about selling coffee—it was about solving a problem for consumers: access to football live transmission that they couldn't otherwise afford at home. And while Sport TV earned its revenue from subscriptions, the cafés earned their right to win by extending customer stays and increasing sales of drinks, food, and other services.

This competitive advantage, however, wasn't permanent. Competitors quickly copied the idea, but the cafés that adopted it first had the upper hand: They built an association in customers' minds. Even after others followed, many customers continued to associate weekend football with the original venue. As one of adidas slogan reminds us: "First never follows."

The lesson is that positioning doesn't have to be complicated or overly scientific. It starts with understanding the dynamics of your customers and offering them something that creates value—even if it's simple.

Positioning, in essence, is about how a company defines itself in a market compared to competitors: what product or service it offers, at what price, and with what advantage.

Returning to the café example: I personally visit two cafés on the same street where my parents live in Portugal. My choice is deliberate, based on their positioning:

At lunchtime, I go to the café closest to the house because it is better organized, has a pleasant terrace, and offers a superior pastry service.

In the evening, I walk to the one further down the street because it has a giant screen showing football, serves dinner, and even makes *francesinhas*.

In both cases, I'm not just consuming the coffee. I'm consuming the *experience as a whole*: the organization, the ambience, the additional services. These "extras" often define the real competitive advantage.

The larger and more complex a market becomes, the harder it is to pinpoint that added value. Broad customer bases bring diverse expectations, making it easy for companies to dilute their positioning.

And that's the risk: Value only exists if it is *perceived* by the customers you serve. A giant screen showing football is meaningless if the local population doesn't care about football. In that case, what was meant as an advantage becomes a wasted investment.

Later, we will analyze the three essential dimensions that define positioning—the customer, the problem, and the value. For now, the key is to appreciate the complexity of being part of a market (whether small or large) and the discipline required to decide: *How should we position ourselves within it?*

It may sound theoretical, but if you think it through, it is not. How often you think of brands and what they tell you, as something that resonates similar way no matter what *ad* you watched, or what product you are looking for. That happens because when brands do it right, they connect what they want to be positioned, and how they tell their story.

Practical Case: Logistics Services

Logistics Services started 10 years ago with a clear goal: to help customers move freight containers from ports to their warehouses. Its unique service is to provide smooth logistics for containers that arrive at the ports of Lisbon, Porto, Algeciras, and Valencia, and then deliver them to clients in the nearby geographical corridor.

The company mainly works with clients whose production comes from faraway places like China, Malaysia, Indonesia, and India. They focus on the textile and retail industries, where supply chains need to be reliable and efficient.

In terms of market potential, logistics companies that move containers between all of Europe's ports could theoretically make about €100 billion a year. The potential market for Logistics Services is estimated to be €5 billion, based on the four ports where the company operates.

Logistics Services makes about €50 million a year right now. This is about 1 percent of the market that is available in the area it covers.

In the example presented, the two main differentiating factors are cost and delivery time. The company's business model is designed to minimize empty truck journeys. Because it only operates between four ports, it can create continuous loops where trucks are almost always loaded.

Take a scenario:

1. A truck loads in Lisbon and unloads at a warehouse in Figueira da Foz.
2. From there, it continues to Porto, where it loads again.
3. It then heads back toward Lisbon, unloading in Santarém before collecting a new load in Lisbon.
4. From Lisbon, it continues south to Algeciras, and so on.

This cycle means fewer unproductive kilometers. Whether a truck is loaded or empty, it incurs costs—fuel, driver wages, wear and tear. Every kilometer driven with cargo is revenue-generating; every empty kilometer is waste. By maximizing loaded journeys, the company increases efficiency and reduces operating costs, strengthening its right to compete on both price and speed.

Although this stage of the book is not about digital transformation solutions, this case illustrates the tight link between business model and technology investment. The company right to win, is the smooth transport between ports, at the lowest cost possible. That said, if the company's right to win lies in minimizing empty kilometers, then its technology focus should be on systems that reinforce that model: route optimization, predictive demand planning, and real-time matching of loads with available trucks. In other words, digital tools should be deployed where they sustain and scale the core advantage.

Another key dimension of positioning is competitor comparison. Knowing your own strengths is not enough; you need to understand how they measure against others in the same space. This is true whether you run a restaurant, a shoe shop, or a logistics business. If customers' needs define the "north star," competitors' offers define the threats.

In logistics, for example, a rival might offer a mobile app that allows customers to track shipments in real time. If your company lacks this feature, even if your prices are lower and delivery faster, customers may drift toward the competitor. Here, the strategic response is defense: investing not to outcompete, but to prevent customers from leaving by matching a minimum set of expectations. Defense protects your advantage (cost and speed) by keeping customers focused on it, rather than being distracted by a competitor's side feature.

The opposite approach is attack: creating unique advantages that others do not yet offer, thereby pulling customers toward you. The café case with Sport TV illustrated this. Being first to offer a valued add-on can build customer loyalty and create a temporary edge, even if competitors eventually replicate it.

Finally, companies must realize that today's competitors are not only the traditional ones. Digital transformation is industrywide. In logistics, for example, new platforms like Uber Freight or Flexport can instantly match shippers and carriers, dramatically lowering barriers to entry and threatening incumbents who rely on older models. Often, the greatest risk comes not from the company down the road, but from disruptive players who change the rules of the market.

A good example of the latter is our Mr. Francis. His business 10 years ago had a much higher barrier to entry. It wasn't easy to open a restaurant overnight and attract new customers. At that stage, it was more common for there to be less need for continuous monitoring of competitors. Today, with the availability of food delivery platforms, there are competitors for Mr. Francis who don't need all the infrastructure he would have needed 10 years ago.

The market is dynamic, and to understand digital transformation is to realize that one of its great benefits, but also risks, is that it removes many of the barriers to entry for new competitors. This means that anyone who settles for a business model that seems unshakable can always run the same risk as Mr. Francis.

The Four Blocks of Digital Transformation

Although digital transformation is at the top of many corporate agendas—and rightly recognized as fundamental—the reality is that failure rates remain incredibly high. Companies embark on ambitious programs only to find that the results fall short of expectations, or worse, that the transformation doesn't truly change the way the business creates value.

Why is this the case? Part of the answer lies in the evolution of markets and consumer habits. There is now a clear perception that companies which fail to digitalize will inevitably lose market relevance and value. This urgency often pushes leadership teams to jump into digital transformation without fully understanding which path to follow. The question becomes: *What kind of digital transformation should we pursue?*

There are many frameworks to structure this process. Some focus on the mechanics of execution—how to manage projects, how to reorganize the company, how to align governance. These are important, and we will cover them later. But even before that, a more fundamental layer must be in place: the structural foundations.

Here, the five pillars (FRAME) we have already discussed play a critical role. They don't prescribe *how* to transform. Instead, they ensure the transformation has the right conditions to succeed. Think of them as the company's health care provider, nutritionist, therapist, and so on. Just as we need some of those to be strong and fit, an organization needs these pillars in place to build the needed behaviors to make the best out of the digital transformation. Without them, even the most sophisticated digital initiatives are unlikely to deliver sustainable impact.

However, once the foundation is secure, transformation cannot remain an abstract ambition. It must take shape in execution. And from a practical perspective, digital transformation can be understood as a set of four main blocks that determine its success. These blocks represent the clearest areas where transformation efforts need to focus—and where risks are most likely to emerge if not carefully managed.

In the next sections, we will explore these four blocks in detail, along with the main risks that threaten digital transformation and how leaders can anticipate them.

These four blocks connect diagnosis to motion. They translate what we've learned about ourselves and our market into the levers we will actually pull during transformation.

The Detail Behind the Four Blocks

Think about someone who wants to run a half-marathon. The goal is clear, but this person needs more than just desire to reach it if they don't work out often and are overweight. It takes planning and self-control in many areas. The five pillars (FRAME) are like the needed preparation: Eat healthy, run x km a week, build a training plan, sleep well, stay hydrated.

Digital transformation is the same. The five pillars (FRAME) make sure that the organization is healthy and ready. We can't run the race, however, without going out there and run. To really "run the race" of change, businesses need to focus on the right things, in addition to the FRAME.

In practice, these levers can be broken down into four main parts:

- Products: how the company has changed what it sells in the digital age
- Operations: changing the way things are done and processes to make them work better at a larger scale

- Technology: which gives you the tools and infrastructure you need
- External Positioning: how the company competes and stands out in the market

On our marathon, the four blocks are the race, the FRAME, is the preparation.

When these four blocks are worked on in line with the five pillars (FRAME), they make up the practical backbone of any digital transformation. They make sure that efforts to change things aren't all over the place but are instead focused on the things that really make a company more competitive and help it grow over time.

Let's take a closer look at each of the four blocks now.

Products

When we talk about a toothbrush or a book, it's easy to imagine something tangible: a physical object that you can hold, touch, and use. But a product is much broader. It is anything a company defines as valuable, that a customer uses to solve a need. That need might be practical, emotional, or social—but the "product" is the structured way the company addresses it. A toothbrush, a flight ticket, a streaming subscription, or a home repair service are all products, even though they are experienced in completely different ways.

This means a product is never just the thing you sell—it is the total experience wrapped around it. When a traveler buys an airline ticket, the flight itself is only one element. The ability to select a seat, bring baggage, board with priority, or cancel with flexibility are also products. Each has its own rules, price, and value to the customer. In logistics, a warehouse is not just space. The real "product" is the way that space is organized, secured, and managed for clients who rely on it.

Modern companies, whether digital start-ups or traditional industries, increasingly adopt this product-oriented mindset. They don't see their business as a bundle of disconnected or undefined services, but as a portfolio of clearly defined products, each with its own market, positioning, and requirements. The question for leaders is therefore not whether you have products, as that is obvious … you do, but whether you truly understand what they are.

Practical Case 1: The plumber's four products

Imagine a small plumbing company. At first glance, it sells "plumbing services." But that description is too broad to manage strategically. When deconstructed, the business actually offers at least four distinct products:

- Repairing pipes in homes
- Ordering and supplying replacement parts
- Inspecting a property's plumbing system
- Installing new pipes in housing developments

Each of these is a different product with its own value proposition, customers, and operational requirements. For example, "emergency pipe repairs" could be defined with a service promise: *arrival within two hours*. That definition instantly sets off questions for the business:

- Can we always guarantee a technician in under two hours?
- How do we filter which calls qualify as true emergencies?
- What price covers the higher costs of urgency?
- Should this product be available everywhere, or only in certain geographies?

This case shows how vague categories become clearer when broken down into products. What looked like a single "plumbing service" is actually multiple products—each requiring its own organization, financial model, and resources.

Practical Case 2: The online jacket seller

Now let's take a small fashion business selling jackets online. At first glance, it has one product: jackets.

But, if you look closer, it has at least two:

- The jacket itself (the physical product)
- The online shop (the digital product that enables access to the jacket)

Customers evaluate both. A buyer might love the jacket's design but abandon the purchase because of a poor online checkout. Another might find the shop excellent but dislike the jacket's quality.

Both the jacket and the platform are separate products, each solving a different customer problem. One addresses fashion and utility, the other addresses convenience, accessibility, and time.

In this sense, you may be wondering why we are discussing this in this chapter that is "looking in the mirror." We are, because it means recognizing that you don't just sell jackets. You sell jackets and an e-commerce experience. Both require investment, both define the customer's perception of your company, and both influence success.

Practical Case 3: The travel agency

Consider a traditional travel agency. For decades, its product was "selling trips." But when we break it down, the products are more specific:
○ Plane tickets
○ Accommodation bookings
○ Excursion packages
○ Insurance
○ Personalized customer support

The agency might think its main product is "holidays." But in practice, customers consume a set of products bundled into one. This becomes even clearer when compared to competitors: Some agencies differentiate by low price, others by exclusive experiences, others by customer care.

Without a clear understanding of these products, an agency risks believing it competes on "holidays" when in fact the competition is happening on insurance prices, refund flexibility, or 24/7 support. Yes, they sell trips, and yes, they sell holidays. That is, however, a package of multiple aspects (products) that ultimate bundle the most competitive solution for a specific customer.

Across these cases, a pattern emerges. Many companies oversimplify their products, believing they sell only one thing when in fact they sell multiple, even if at times, they don't even get paid for some. Each of those products has its own customer expectations, pricing models, and operational implications.

Looking at yourself through the "products block" requires stripping away vague definitions and asking:

○ What exactly are we selling?
○ How many products do we really have?
○ What components define them (features, services, channels)?
○ Are they financially viable in the way we promise them?

Only by answering these questions can a company understand the true scope of what it offers, and the risks or opportunities hidden in its product portfolio.

Understanding products is not about designing new ones or adding more features. That comes later in the ASCEND journey. In this stage, it is about seeing clearly what your products already are, how customers perceive them, and what it takes internally to deliver them.

A digital transformation will fail if the company doesn't fully understand its products in this deeper sense. Technology, processes, and investments only make sense if they are aligned with clearly defined products. Uber doesn't sell an app—it sells transportation as a product. Amazon doesn't sell just goods—it sells convenience and reliability as a product.

The clearer a company is about what it "actually sells," the easier it becomes to understand how to transform it successfully.

Operations

The operations of a business are what keeps it running. When things are going well, they are often not noticed, but when something goes wrong, they are very clear.

In football, they are the ones we call "the piano carriers." They aren't the stars on the front page, but they are the ones who make sure the team works as a unit. They don't get much attention in companies, but they are what keeps the system running. If operations aren't in line with strategy and product, digital transformation could just be a facade: a smooth front end that falls apart when promises aren't kept.

When you look at yourself, you should look at your operations the same way you look at your products, markets, and technology. You need to ask:

- Are the processes that support what we sell set up to keep the promise we make?
- Do our suppliers, logistics, and internal processes make our offer stronger or weaker?
- Are we only looking at the customer experience at the point of sale when we measure success?

These questions are not just ideas. They directly decide if transformation builds trust or distrust.

Practical Case: Building Materials Co. and a promise broken

A large building-materials distributor launched an ambitious digital strategy in 2022: move 95 percent of orders online by 2027. To anchor trust, leadership set a clear KPI: deliver 98 percent of orders on the promised date. The company invested heavily in its digital commerce platform. By 2023, adoption was strong. Over 70 percent of clients were ordering digitally, drawn by convenience, transparency, and promotional incentives. At first glance, the strategy seemed to be working.

The problem: Customer complaints rose dramatically. Common issues included:

- Deliveries arriving late or incomplete
- Billing errors tied to special-order conditions
- Promises made online not reflecting operational capacity

By late 2024, fulfillment performance had fallen to 88 percent, far below the 98 percent KPI. The number of customer complaints had tripled compared to 2022.

The postmortem showed that the product (the promise of digital convenience) and the operations (the ability to deliver consistently on that promise) were not in sync.

- ○ Same promise, different levels of difficulty. The platform handled all orders the same way, promising the same delivery times for both regular and "special" orders that needed cutting, sequencing, or delivery off route. In terms of how they worked, these two groups were very different.
- ○ Manual bottlenecks hidden behind a digital front. Even though the order capture was digital, a lot of the fulfillment flow still relied on paper-based approvals, phone calls, and manual scheduling. There was a digital promise that depended on analog execution.
- ○ Incentives that aren't aligned. Sales teams were rewarded for using digital tools, not for delivering on time. The company was happy that more people were ordering online, but they didn't notice that trust was going down.

The Effect

By the middle of 2025, some important contractors who made up 15 percent of revenue moved some of their business to competitors who made clearer and more reliable delivery promises. Reputation surveys showed that people thought the company was less reliable, even customers who had never had a problem. The difference between what was promised and what actually happened had become a make it or break it situation.

This example illustrates the necessity of evaluating oneself through an operational lens prior to, rather than subsequent to, a digital transformation.

- The promise is only as strong as the people who carry the piano. No matter how well the sales channel works, operations are what make the promise last in the real world.
- Trust from customers is weak. One broken promise can break dozens of successful deliveries. Reputation builds up over time, but failure happens right away.
- It's worse to have digital tools that aren't ready to use than to not have any at all. It raises hopes that you can't meet, which makes disappointment worse.

Customers today don't just compare you to your direct competitors. Even if you're in a completely different field, a contractor who orders cement will compare your service to how reliable Amazon deliveries are. People don't just compare a restaurant's delivery service to other restaurants; they also compare it to Uber Eats and Glovo. This benchmarking across industries makes operations more important. Later we will talk a bit more about this principle, where at times your competitor is not the one that sells the same product but rather the one who addresses similar problem, even though with a different product.

If you say that delivery will take 20 minutes, but it always takes 60 minutes, customers will quickly stop coming back. The same goes for materials, logistics, retail, and any other field.

If operations aren't ready to back up the promise, digital transformation won't work. To look at yourself operationally means asking the hard questions:

- Are our people, processes, and systems all working together to keep our promises?
- Where are the gaps between what we sell and what we can always deliver?
- Are we rewarding the use of technology or the dependability of our operations?

You can only build a change that makes your business stronger, not weaker, when you have this clear picture.

Technology

When people think of digital transformation, their first thought is almost always technology. It's undeniable that technology plays a central role, but it is not the transformation itself. Technology is the enabler, the accelerator, the set of tools that allows strategy, products, and operations to come to life. Without clarity on these, technology can easily become just another cost—or worse, a distraction.

This block is also where we see the greatest difference between micro and small companies on one side, and medium and large companies on the other. In small businesses, technology is often an afterthought, used in a limited or fragmented way. By contrast, larger organizations usually have more formal decision-making processes: software architecture reviews, business architecture functions, or IT governance bodies that evaluate investments. These practices exist for a reason: Technology is not neutral. Every tool you introduce shapes how people work, how fast processes run, and how customers experience your service.

A real example illustrates this well. A few years ago, I received a request for help from a friend who owned a local business. Despite generating more than half a million in revenue, the company had persistent cash flow problems and rarely ended the year in profit. The issue was not lack of customers, but the way the finances were managed. The transactions were run entirely on paper: lists of prices, invoices, purchase records, and inventory notes scattered across piles of paper. Any attempt to get a clear picture of the company's financial situation required hours—sometimes days—of manual consolidation. By the time the numbers were clear, decisions were already outdated.

This case is far from isolated. Studies show that a significant percentage of micro and small business leaders remain unaware of how technology can help them manage more effectively. When this happens, the problem isn't the absence of technology itself, but the absence of technological literacy—the ability to see how even simple tools could unlock better and faster decisions.

Practical Case: A tale of two companies

Imagine two companies of very different sizes, both facing challenges in managing their operations.

- ○ Company A is a small furniture shop with five employees. All inventory and orders are tracked manually in notebooks and Excel sheets. The owner spends several hours a week trying to reconcile stock with sales and often discovers errors only after customers complain about delays.
- ○ Company B is a multinational with thousands of employees. It operates several ERP systems and has an IT architecture team

responsible for evaluating new software. While its complexity is higher, there is also a structured process for deciding which technology supports the company's strategy and processes.

Both companies use technology. But the way they do it, and the role technology plays in their ability to make decisions, is entirely different. One relies on manual processes that limit visibility and create risk; the other has frameworks in place that reduce the chance of blind spots.

External Positioning

Even if a company has the best product in the world, runs perfectly, and uses the latest technology, it will never reach its full potential if customers don't know about it. External positioning connects what you sell to how the market sees and uses it. It's all about being seen, trusted, and turning visitors into customers. Without this bridge, even the best internal plans fail without anyone knowing.

This isn't about metrics that make you feel good, like likes, shares, or impressions. It's about reaching the right customers in the right way, making sure that attention leads to interest and interest leads to sales. The reasoning is clear: Noise is awareness without conversion, and conversion is impossible without awareness.

When you look at yourself from the outside, you have to ask tough questions like:

- Do our customers know we exist, and do they understand what we can do for them?
- Are we easy to find in the places where our customers make decisions?
- Do we only look at engagement to see how well we're doing, or do we also look at actual results like orders, contracts, and loyalty?

Are we telling stories that people can relate to, or are we just making content for the sake of making content?

Practical Case: Fashion brand lost in the noise

A new fashion company from Portugal started in 2023. It sells eco-friendly streetwear made from recycled materials. Its product was good: It had a trendy design, eco-friendly fabrics, and prices that were competitive. Operations were well organized: Deliveries were on time, customer service was good, and suppliers could grow with the business. But by 2025, sales had leveled off at €300,000 a year, which was well below industry standards.

The issue: The brand spent a lot of money on social media—over €5,000 a month on Instagram ads; their posts got tens of thousands of likes but only led to fewer than 30 orders a month. Most of the engagement came from people who lived outside of the brand's shipping areas.

Analysis

- The wrong focus: Campaigns that were focused on getting people to see them, not on making sales. A lot of "likes" made it look like they were doing well, but it didn't have much of an effect on their finances.
- Bad targeting: Ads reached people all over the world, but shipping limits kept a lot of potential buyers from buying. This mismatch made people angry and cost money.
- No clear plot: Posts focused on how things looked ("look at this outfit") but didn't explain why they were different, which was the sustainability angle.
- Competitor overshadowing: The story was mostly about bigger international eco-fashion brands, which drowned out the start-up's voice.

Effect

By the end of 2025, the cash reserves were low. The brand could have gone out of business in 18 months if it didn't get better external positioning. The problem wasn't the product; it was that it wasn't well known in the right markets.

Practical Case: The logistics company that nobody knew

Contrast this with a midsize logistics company (annual revenue: €50M) offering highly competitive freight solutions between Iberian ports. Internally, the business was efficient, and cost optimized. Customers loved the service *when they found it*. But market research revealed that 70 percent of potential clients in their region had never even heard of the company, while competitors with weaker services had stronger visibility.

Analysis

- The company focused marketing on industry fairs and cold calls, ignoring digital channels where procurement managers increasingly searched for logistics partners.
- Website visibility was minimal, Google searches for "logistics Iberia freight" barely showed the company in the first 10 pages.
- Social presence was limited to a static LinkedIn page, updated only twice a year.

Impact

The company was playing at 1 percent market share in a €5B addressable market. Their external positioning was the bottleneck: They had the trucks, the people, the processes, but not the visibility to scale.

Lessons from the Cases

These examples highlight why external positioning is not optional—it is the oxygen of business growth.

Attention ≠ Success. Empty metrics create illusions. What matters is conversion, followed by fulfilled promise

External positioning is about relevance. It's not only about being seen but being seen by the right audience, in the right places, with the right message.

Narrative matters. Customers buy stories as much as they buy products. The sustainability story in the fashion case, or the efficiency story in logistics, are differentiators that must be told clearly.

Competitors define context. Your visibility is relative. If your competitors dominate digital channels and you don't, you're effectively invisible.

External positioning is the outer layer of the four digital transformation blocks (technology, products, operations, positioning). It is what touches the customer first and most visibly. The harsh truth: If they don't know you, they won't buy from you.

But looking at yourself here is not about rushing to hire a marketing agency or flooding social media with content. It's about recognizing:

- Where are you actually visible today?
- Do customers know your story?
- Do you know how much of your engagement really converts into revenue?
- Are you chasing likes, or building trust and demand?

Digital transformation without external positioning is like shouting in an empty room. The message must leave the walls of the company and meet customers where they are.

In short, connecting these four blocks helps define the company as a whole and apply digital transformation in a more sustained and consistent way. Each block is interdependent:

- **Products** crystallize the value the company offers and define what must be delivered consistently to customers.
- **Operations** ensure that what is promised is achievable, turning ambition into execution.
- **Technology** enables the design of better products, ensures operations are more efficient, and connects processes with suppliers and partners.
- **External positioning** makes sure customers know about the offer and see it as relevant, attractive, and trustworthy.

When these four areas are disconnected, transformation risks becoming fragmented, producing isolated wins but systemic weaknesses. But when they work together, the result is not only better products or better marketing but a company that moves forward coherently—offering what customers want, delivering it reliably, and ensuring the market recognizes its value.

Risks for the Digital Transformation Process

Some studies[7] point to a high number (between 65 percent and 85 percent) of companies that fail to achieve the expected results from their digital transformation, especially because they are unaware of the potential of technology and new business models, in the most optimistic cases. In other words, seven or eight companies out of every 10 that try to transform don't achieve the results they set out to achieve.

As a rule, risk management is crucial to the success of any project or program, since it is these risks, when they become reality, that often lead to projects running into problems. Those who manage risks are closer to preventing delays and the problems they cause. A digital transformation process is no different. Understanding the most common risks helps you realize where to focus to prevent them from becoming a reality.

Returning to our half-marathon analogy: It's sometimes difficult to manage everything you need to ensure that you're fit, healthy and energized for race day. There are various factors that can, in one way or another, impact all our planning and jeopardize all the work we've done so far. The digital transformation is no different. Even with very detailed planning, there are always risks that must be monitored. In this case, I've grouped them into five main groups, which are the most common.

Here's an explanation of the five major groups.

1. **Unclear definitions**

   Perhaps the most common risk is the inability to clearly define what it means to digitalize a particular business. As discussed in earlier chapters, companies don't even have a plan, some don't know they need one, and others confuse digital transformation with simply implementing a new IT system. But buying a system is not a transformation. Without a clear definition (business models, of the role of technology, of the markets they aim to serve), companies risk investing in tools without direction.

---

[7]Barry Libert, Megan Beck, and Yoram Wind, "7 Questions to Ask Before Your Next Digital Transformation," *Harvard Business Review*, March 2016, https://hbr.org/2016/03/7-questions-to-ask-before-your-next-digital-transformation.

2. **Overfocusing in the technology aspect**

   The second risk comes from equating "digital" with "IT." Because the word digital has long been associated with systems or online channels, many leaders fall into the trap of seeing digital transformation as a purely technical endeavor. But as history shows, many disruptive players have outpaced incumbents not by buying better technology, but by redesigning models, experiences, and processes around the customer. Companies that focus only on technology risk simply digitalizing the same old problems.

3. **The influence of culture**

   Peter Drucker's[8] famous phrase, "Culture eats strategy for breakfast," is particularly true here. The larger the company, the harder it is to shift learned behaviors. Digital transformation often fails not because the strategy is wrong but because the culture resists change. In many medium-to-large companies, if culture and behavioral change are not addressed, digital initiatives can create rifts between management layers, slowing or derailing transformation entirely.

4. **Vision or lacking one**

   Markets under pressure often force leaders into short-term thinking. "Short-term blindness" is one of the biggest risks: Decisions made to address immediate problems may undermine the company's ability to thrive in the medium-to-long term. Over time, the accumulation of short-sighted fixes becomes a structural obstacle to transformation. The paradox is clear: Digital transformation requires long-term vision, but leaders under pressure often lack the bandwidth to sustain it.

5. **The role of management**

   Finally, management itself can be a source of risk. Poorly structured leadership teams, lack of alignment, or an unfocused portfolio of initiatives can cripple execution. Many companies attempt to do too many things at once, stretching resources thin and diluting impact. Transformation requires alignment at the top, clear prioritization, and disciplined management. Without these, even the

---

[8]"About Peter Drucker," Drucker Institute, accessed August 31, 2025. https://drucker.institute/about-peter-drucker.

best strategies and technologies end up failing when it comes to execution, especially when first challenges arise. One of the interesting challenges that leaders face, is their unintentional (most of the times) approach to oversimply. A big disruptive technology-enabled transformation, called "system implementation." This happens most of times, due to fear of its impact, due to fear of what it may entail in terms of change management, and so on. The bad news? It doesn't make any difference what we call it. The challenges faced will be the exact same ones. The more fear we let take over, and with that, apply some intrinsic defensive mechanisms, the more complex we make, even though we wanted to make it simpler.

These five groups of risks exemplify some of the pitfalls that companies encounter when thinking about digital transformation processes. Many are complex to resolve, and some require drastic change across structures, behaviors, and leadership.

From my experience, when I see success stories, they always share one feature: Transformation is treated as whole-organization change, not as "digital in isolation." In these cases, leaders understood that transformation is multidisciplinary and transversal. They looked at their business models, their culture, their processes, their customer engagement—and orchestrated all of it together.

Interestingly, technology itself is often the simplest component. The hardest part, by far, is the human component: culture, vision, and leadership.

It is therefore less important to ask, "Which digital transformation should I choose?" and more important to ask, "How do I manage it holistically, while keeping focus on what really matters: vision, products, operations, external positioning, and culture?" Always with an eye on the risks that can undermine execution.

The combination of the five pillars (FRAME), the four blocks of digital transformation (Products, Operations, Technology, External Positioning), and the five major risks together create what I call the *Digital Transformation Foundation* (illustrated in Figure 3.1).

This foundation does not prescribe a specific path. Rather, it highlights the areas of focus: where readiness must be built, where implementation should concentrate, and where risks must be anticipated. For

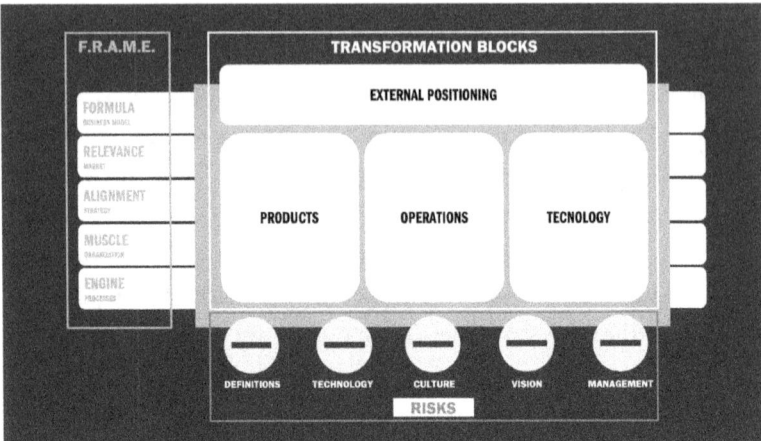

Figure 3.1 The digital transformation foundation

leaders, the most important message is this: Digital transformation is a multidisciplinary orchestration. Its success lies not in technology alone, but in the ability to align people, processes, culture, and vision while carefully managing the risks that will inevitably emerge.

As you may have understood throughout this past chapters, we spent some time learning about us (the company) and its surroundings, but in most of the areas we tackled, we never lost sight of our customer, even when look at ourselves. I hope some of you may have raised the conflicting question, "If it is all about our customers, what about our employees?" If you did, that is a very pertinent question. You will hear my answer in much more detail later—but who said "Customer" is "only" the one who buys (one way or another) our products?

CHAPTER 4

The Understanding of Your Customers

The customer is, without a shadow of a doubt, the central component in any digital transformation process. Every decision, from strategy to execution, must ultimately serve one goal: to create or improve a product that fulfills a customer's need.

However, many companies lose sight of this. They become what I call *channeled*—so focused on their internal "plumbing" that they forget who the most important part of this all equation is. Companies must look inward and manage their structures—but it cannot become the limit of leadership thinking.

A business without customers is not a business at all. Without them, there is no market or organization, and without a market or an organization, there is no business. That is why the customer must always sit at the very center of any digital transformation effort.

This also means learning to deprioritize. Companies must stop investing time and energy in things that add little value to customers. The difficulty is that leaders often believe these activities are vital for the company's health, even when they are not. And as organizations grow-in-size and complexity, leaders increasingly struggle to see the company as an integrated piece. Returning to the *digital transformation foundation* discussed earlier, it is common in larger firms for different leaders to perceive the same components in fundamental different ways. This misalignment creates internal friction, where energy is consumed in alignment meetings rather than in creative processes, the unique space where true customer value can be thought through.

Placing the customer at the center sounds complex, but as I heard once in a movie ("Bleed for This"), the biggest lie we are told is that it is not that simple. It is. It requires leaders to step outside themselves and adopt the customer's perspective. For instance, a restaurateur redesigning their dining room must ask: *If I walk into this room, what do I feel?* or *If I don't want to order anything else, how can I avoid being interrupted?* These are not theoretical questions—they are customer-centered ones. The same applies in a larger customers. It requires even more from senior leaders, to lead by example, make shaper decisions, drag less meetings, entertain less "alignments." If the center is the customer, that shall be what sets the tone and the urgency, rather the intrinsic corporate complexity of decision making.

Digital adds new dimensions to customer interaction, but it should never be the *only* lens. Physical interaction remains just as important. A friendly smile from the owner of a bakery, or the way a shopkeeper remembers a customer's name, can be as transformative as a mobile app. A simple "good morning" to an employee in the corridor, a genuine "how are you?" and waiting for the long answer, can be as effective as a good "company internal site," or a renewed "finance platform." A quicker decision that benefits the employees even though brings little self-gain, or quicker test of a new product in the market, can be more effective than a large system implementation or a massive campaign. We will be better in tackling the big customer centricity, the second we manage to overcome the "little things" that can be as impactful to start with.

In essence, customer centricity is nothing more than a discipline of constantly asking: *What would a customer ask or feel in this situation? What is the right thing to do for this customer?* Leaders who fail to understand their customers inevitably struggle to create value. And this is not a "soft" principle, it is a fundamental business rule. Leaders must remember we don't work for our managers, or our self-promotion. We work for our customers.

Consider B2B companies, where traditional sales models still rely in many cases on personal relationships. The stereotype of the successful salesperson is the one who closes deals over a round of golf or a good bottle of wine. That form of selling requires proximity, time, and social skill. But it is increasingly at odds with digital transformation. This does not mean that relationships no longer matter—salespeople will always need to build trust—but the *majority* of sales now depend on technology, data, and personalization, not golf games. How to adjust?

In traditional face-to-face selling, the salesperson's deep knowledge of the customer is what drives success. They adapt in real-time to humor, tone, or body language. In digital channels, much of that human nuance disappears, replaced by algorithms and automated journeys. This shift highlights a paradox: No matter how sophisticated technology becomes, *humanization* remains what defines us. Designing technology without humanization risks creating cold, impersonal interactions that fail to build loyalty. The challenge for companies, therefore, is to design digital systems that embed empathy and personalization into their very core.

The trend is undeniable. Even before the pandemic, customer habits were shifting steadily toward digital-first interactions. COVID-19 merely accelerated what was already happening: Digital channels are no longer a complement but often the default, even when embedded in physical ones.

For this reason, understanding the customer is the anchor of digital transformation. In this chapter, we will explore three dimensions that help companies put customers where they belong—at the center:

- Who is my customer? Identifying clearly who we serve
- Success point: understanding customer problems and how to solve them
- Customer journey: mapping every interaction, from discovery to after-sales support

Only when these three elements are addressed with discipline can digital transformation fulfill its true promise: to create real, sustainable value for the customer.

Who Is the Customer?

Finding out who a customer is much harder than it seems at first. This is especially true for businesses that focus on consumers, where the range is wide, varied, and often hard to predict. Remember my comment in the previous chapter? If you were thinking that customers for me, are solely the ones who buy products, this is a good chapter to have an even closer look.

We usually think of a customer as someone who buys something or gets a service and pays for it, either with money or by doing something for someone else. But that's not the whole story. A customer is more than just the person who buys something from you. A customer is often anyone, inside or outside the company, who gets something of value from it, like a product or service.

So far, we've mostly talked about the outside market and the end customers who builds that market. And really, there is no market without customers, and there is no company without a market. But it's also true that there can't be a product without the people who design, build, ship, and support it. In this way, the systems, tools, and services that help employees do their jobs, are products needed for the internal customers. The customers that in a way, play that vital role in delivering newer experiences to the end customer, the customers who can make it or break it when it comes down to fulfilling promises.

Think about a business that makes parts for machines. Who buys from it? The obvious answer is the people who buy those parts to use in their own products or processes. But just as important are the employees in procurement, logistics, distribution, and after-sales who depend on internal systems and services to make sure those parts are delivered on time and in the right quality.

The same thing is true for businesses that have technology or digital departments. These teams make tools for both internal and external customers. For example, they make a logistics app for delivery teams, a finance dashboard for controllers, or a customer portal that makes things easier for support staff.

This brings us to an important difference:

- End customers are people or companies (through people) who buy and use the company's products.
- Internal customers are employees and departments that need tools or services from the company to deliver value to end customers.

This difference is not just for academics; it is very important. Because they make money, bigger businesses often only pay attention to their end customers. But ignoring internal customers is dangerous. The company won't be able to keep its promises to the market if its workers don't have the tools, systems, or support they need to do their jobs. It will be hard for a company to stay in business if it can't deliver on time, even when there is demand.

To really know who the customer is, you need to go beyond this simple classification. The end customer is still a fundamental important part of digital transformation, but whether the transformation works depends on whether internal customers are ready and able to do their jobs.

You may wonder, if customers are that center, how can those be better identified?

Leaders can use different methods, often together, to better identify and define their customers:

- Segmentation: Clustering customers into groups based on things they have in common, like their age, gender, or buying habits
- Personas: Creating detailed models of specific customer types to make them more human and help you understand what they want, what frustrates them, and what they need
- Jobs to Be Done: Instead of focusing on who the customer is, focus on the problem they want to solve and find out which groups have the same problem.

Each method gives you a different point of view. Segmentation makes things clear on a large scale, personas add empathy and detail, and jobs-to-be-done shows the real functional problems that affect customer decisions. When used together, they make a powerful set of tools for answering the deceptively simple question, "Who is my customer?"

Let's have a look more in detail.

Segmentation

For many companies—particularly larger ones—segmentation is a core process in defining their commercial strategy. At its essence, segmentation means dividing a market into groups of customers who share common characteristics, allowing the organization to target them more effectively.

Take, for example, a company selling printing materials. It might initially define two obvious segments:

- Students—individuals across different levels of education who frequently need printing materials for assignments or projects
- Teachers—who share a similar need, but at a different level of demand

This is only the beginning. Each of these broad categories can be broken into subsegments: higher education students versus secondary school students, university professors versus primary or secondary school teachers. In theory, segmentation can go into infinite layers of detail, the key is stopping at the level that gives the clearest perception of the end customer being analyzed.

The concept itself is not new. Wendell R. Smith first introduced the idea of market segmentation in his 1956 paper "Product Differentiation and Market Segmentation as Alternative Marketing Strategies".[9] At the time, markets were less diverse and more homogeneous, so a generalized approach to consumers was sufficient. Since then, segmentation has evolved into a core discipline of marketing strategy. Caroline Tynan[10] has also contributed influential work on market segmentation, expanding its relevance to modern contexts.

Common Types of Market Segmentation

There are many approaches to segment customers, here I present four those, and sometimes they use more than one at a time:

- Demographic: based on things like age, gender, salary, or job
- Psychographic: less tangible, focuses on values, lifestyles, and personalities. For instance, someone who likes to stay inside probably won't be the main buyer of beach towels.

---

[9]Wendell R. Smith, "Product Differentiation and Market Segmentation as Alternative Marketing Strategies," *Journal of Marketing* 21, no. 1 (July 1956): 3–8.
[10]Caroline A. Tynan and Jennifer Drayton, "Market Segmentation," *Journal of Marketing Management* 2, no. 3 (1987): 301–35. https://doi.org/10.1080/0267 257X.1987.9964020.

- Behavioral: based on patterns of how people act, like how often they buy something or how loyal they are to a brand
- Geographical: putting customers into groups based on where they live. For example, suppliers of equipment for preserving fresh fish would probably focus on coastal areas.

There are more though. For example, price-based segmentation (Ryanair versus Lufthansa), seasonality (beach products in summer), or even segmentation by distribution channel.

Why Segmentation Matters

Segmentation is not only about defining *what to do*—it is equally powerful in clarifying *what not to do*. Like a songwriter who writes a ballad for a pop audience rather than fans of heavy metal, a company must recognize which groups are *not* the right fit for its product and avoid wasting resources trying to reach them.

For companies in digital transformation, segmentation becomes even more important. It allows leaders to align strategy with the expectations of specific groups. Consider a bookselling company: The rise of digital formats has already changed the playing field, but what comes next? If the target is digitally savvy readers, the strategy cannot stop at simply selling books online. Segmentation insights may reveal opportunities to create a platform that offers a *reading experience*: online conversations with authors, the ability to annotate and save notes, or even book-as-a-service models—renting a book for 48 hours, much like streaming video content on Netflix or Amazon.

The underlying principle is this: Customers do not only compare your product with direct competitors. They compare across industries, against the best experiences they encounter elsewhere. Someone buying digital books will benchmark you against Amazon or Apple just as easily as against your closest rival. The bar is set by the very best. This is not only true to end customers but also to internal customers. Companies need the best talent, and to retain the best talent, they also compare with other companies. All things matter.

Limitations of Segmentation

Despite its value, segmentation is not without risks. Traditional segmentation focuses heavily on the *profile* of the customer, not necessarily their *needs*. This creates an assumption that people with similar characteristics share the same problems, which can lead to oversimplification. In the digital age—where personalization is increasingly expected—this limitation becomes more problematic.

To counteract this, companies now rely heavily on data. Every digital interaction—search habits, purchases, preferences, even reaction times—helps refine the understanding of customers at an individual level. Segmentation remains useful, but in practice it is now complemented with data-driven personalization.

Finally, although segmentation is often discussed in the context of *end customers*, it can also be applied internally. Grouping internal customers (employees or departments) by their characteristics or needs can help design better processes and systems, especially when building digital tools for internal use.

In simple terms, segmentation is about finding the patterns that matter—whether in markets or inside organizations—and building strategies around them. It is both a map of where to go, and a warning of where *not* to waste energy.

Personas

While segmentation groups customers into categories, personas[11] give those groups a face, a story, and a voice. A persona is a fictional character that represents a set of shared attributes among a group of consumers—demographics, behaviors, motivations, and even frustrations—crafted in such a way that it feels like a real person.

The concept of personas in marketing can be traced back to Professor Angus Jenkinson[12] in 1993–1994, who first used the approach as a

---

[11]John S. Pruitt and Jonathan Grudin, "Personas: Practice and Theory," in *Proceedings of the 2003 Conference on Designing for User Experiences (DUX '03)* (Association for Computing Machinery, 2003), 1–15, https://doi.org/10.1145/997078.997089.
[12]Angus Jenkinson, "Beyond Segmentation," *Journal of Targeting, Measurement and Analysis for Marketing* 3, no. 1 (1994): 60–72.

practical way to humanize customer data. Instead of seeing consumers as anonymous clusters of numbers, personas allow businesses to imagine them as individuals with personalities, preferences, and decision-making styles.

An Example of a Persona

Consider this fictional profile:

> *John, 25 years old. He loves surfing, skateboarding, and snowboarding. He has little patience for television and is indifferent to football. He enjoys vegetarian food, though he is not fully vegetarian. He is not especially passionate about technology, but he owns the latest iPhone.*

This description may seem casual, but it has strong meanings. John is a young, health-conscious, adventure-seeking consumer who uses technology in a moderate way. For marketers, this means: Don't waste time and money trying to sell him a PlayStation (he's not interested).

- Think about selling him a wetsuit or sports gear (very relevant).
- Make healthy summer foods look like appealing options (fit with lifestyle).

By giving these traits a face, companies go from statistical abstraction to real empathy. The persona reminds the business that the data is made up of real people with feelings, habits, and contradictions.

Beyond Consumer Markets

Although personas are most common in B2C contexts, they are equally valuable in B2B environments. For instance, a consultancy firm seeking to win clients might build personas for the different decision makers within a target company:

- CFO Carla: analytical, focused on cost reduction, prefers reports full of financial projections and evidence

- HR Director Alex: values people-centric outcomes, prefers stories, testimonials, and case studies
- CEO Maria: visionary, focused on long-term impact, more receptive to bold strategy and big-picture benefits

By aligning communication styles, tone, and even the sales pitch to these personas, the consultancy can reduce the margin for error, strengthen relationships, and create a more personalized commercial approach. Instead of "one-size-fits-all" messaging, every stakeholder feels that the service was *designed with them in mind.*

Why Personas Matter in Digital Transformation

In the context of digital transformation, personas serve as a bridge between customer data and customer empathy. With digitalization, companies often find themselves drowning in quantitative data—clicks, dwell time, purchase frequency—but struggling to translate that data into insights that feel human. Personas reintroduce the human dimension into the design of digital platforms, marketing campaigns, and even internal tools.

Think of a company designing a mobile app. Without personas, the design team might focus solely on technical features. With personas, they ask questions like:

- *Would "John" find the navigation intuitive?*
- *Would "CFO Carla" trust this dashboard enough to make decisions?*
- *Would "Alex" feel supported by the tone of the language?*

This type of framing forces empathy and prioritizes user experience over purely technical efficiency.

Criticisms and Limitations

Even though people like them, personas have their critics. The biggest problems are:

- Oversimplification: Making complicated customer situations into a few made-up characters can leave out important details.

- Static nature: Markets change, and if personas aren't updated, they may quickly become useless.
- Subjectivity: If not done well, personas might be based on stereotypes or guesses instead of real data.
- Execution difficulty: In large or varied markets, it can be hard to make actionable personas, which makes it hard for businesses to use them.

Best practice says that when making personas, you should use both quantitative data (like analytics, surveys, and CRM systems) and qualitative data (like interviews and ethnographic research). This will help you avoid these risks. Also, personas should be seen as living documents that need to be looked at and improved on a regular basis as markets change, and customer behaviors change.

Jobs to Be Done

Unlike segmentation or personas, which focus on *who the customer is*, the Jobs to Be Done (JTBD) theory focuses on *what problem the customer needs to solve*. It is less about customer identity and more about customer intent—what they are "hiring" a product or service to do for them.

The JTBD theory is closely associated with Clayton Christensen,[13] professor at Harvard Business School, who argued that customers rarely buy products for their own sake. Instead, they "hire" them as tools to achieve an outcome.

A Simple Example

Imagine you need to hang a picture on the wall. You go to the store and buy a drill. But if we pause for a moment—did you actually want a drill? No. What you wanted was a hole in the wall to hang the frame. The drill is not the real goal; it is only a temporary solution. If tomorrow a company invents an adhesive system that holds a picture as securely as a

---

[13]C. M. Christensen, T. Hall, K. Dillon, and D. S. Duncan, "Know Your Customers, Jobs to Be Done," *Harvard Business Review*, September 2016, 10.

drilled screw—without the noise, dust, or effort—you might very well choose that product instead, perhaps even paying more.

This is the essence of JTBD: Customers are not loyal to solutions; they are loyal to problems being solved effectively.

From Product to Problem

Traditional companies often compete by improving the product itself—lighter drills, faster drills, cheaper drills. But a JTBD approach flips the perspective: Instead of refining the drill, focus on the *job*—securely hanging a picture. This opens the door for completely different categories of innovation, even outside the industry's original boundaries.

This logic explains why disruptive companies often emerge not from within industries, but from outside them. They focus on *problems*, not *products*.

Technology Examples: Uber and Airbnb

Two of the most cited cases of JTBD in action are Uber and Airbnb:

- Uber: Taxis offered transportation. Uber reframed the job as *mobility and convenience*. The company realized people don't care about the taxi per se—they care about moving from A to B quickly, safely, and predictably. By solving *mobility*, Uber competes not only with taxis but with car ownership itself. For many urban dwellers, the convenience of calling an Uber is enough to abandon the need for a private car.
- Airbnb: Hotels sell rooms. Airbnb reframed the job as *temporary accommodation*. People don't "want a hotel"; they want a place to stay when away from home. By focusing on the underlying job rather than the traditional product, Airbnb positioned itself to compete with both hotels and online booking platforms, creating an entirely new category of accommodation experience.

Both companies illustrate Christensen's principle: Customers are not buying a category; they are hiring a solution to a problem.

JTBD and Digital Transformation

In the context of digital transformation, JTBD is particularly relevant because it fosters innovation that cuts across traditional boundaries. Digital tools often make it possible to solve problems in ways that were previously unimaginable:

- Instead of designing better physical maps, companies created Google Maps to solve the job of navigation.
- Instead of making better DVDs, Netflix solved the job of "entertainment on demand."

By focusing on jobs, organizations avoid the trap of digitalizing existing inefficiencies. They instead identify opportunities for disruptive solutions that can transform entire industries.

Complementarity with Segmentation and Personas

JTBD does not replace segmentation or personas. Rather, it complements them:

- Segmentation identifies *groups of people* with similar traits.
- Personas humanize those traits into relatable archetypes.
- Jobs to Be Done cuts across traits and groups, focusing instead on the *problem being solved*.

For example, segmentation might tell you your customer is a "25–30-year-old male, university-educated, urban resident." A persona might describe him as "John, the young surfer who values health and lifestyle." But JTBD asks: *What job is John trying to get done?* If John wants to travel easily around the city, he might hire Uber. If he wants to connect with friends abroad, he might hire WhatsApp. The job is the real driver of his decision, regardless of who he is demographically.

Criticisms and Limitations

While powerful, JTBD also has challenges:

1. Abstractness—Jobs can sometimes be defined too broadly (e.g., "I want to be happy"), making them difficult to operationalize.
2. Prioritization difficulty—Customers may have multiple jobs, and it's not always clear which are most urgent or valuable.
3. Execution risk—Knowing the job doesn't automatically mean creating the right solution; poor design can still fail.

To fix this, businesses often use outcome-driven innovation methods, qualitative interviews, and ethnographic research to clearly define the "job" in terms that can be acted on.

Jobs to Be Done is less about who the customer is and more about what makes them choose. It tells leaders to stop being so obsessed with their products and instead think about the main problems that customers are trying to solve.

This point of view is very helpful in digital transformation. It helps businesses not only make their current products and services better but also change the way industries work, come up with new categories, and come up with disruptive innovations.

Segmentation, personas, and JTBD make up a set of tools that help businesses understand their customers from three different points of view: who they are, what they stand for, and what problems they need to solve.

The Success Point: Customer, Problem, and Value

The product is not defined by the features we design into it but by the way customers fall in love with it, relate to it, and understand it.

Too often, the digitalization agenda is driven by a narrow urge to "do something with technology," without a clear strategic anchor. A company invests in digital platforms, apps, or systems, but if the underlying product is in decline or the market is shrinking, technology alone will not change the trajectory.

Digital transformation must be understood as a holistic process: analyzing the company, its environment, its strategy, and the customer needs it seeks to address. Technology is a critical enabler, but it cannot be a substitute for vision. Based on my experience, a digital transformation should never begin unless the company is able to define a medium- to long-term vision—a north star against which every decision can be tested. Without this anchor, transformation risks becoming a scattered collection of disconnected initiatives.

So how do we move from vision to meaningful transformation? This is where the concept of the "Point of Success" comes in.

A company does not exist simply because its founders, owners, or managers want it to. It exists because it creates products or services that solve real problems for customers, and in doing so generates value.

The Point of Success sits at the intersection of three critical elements:

- Customer—Who are we serving?
- Problem—What problem, challenge, or job are they trying to solve?
- Value—What tangible or intangible benefit do they gain if we solve that problem effectively?

When these three elements overlap, companies find the foundation of their relevance. They not only position themselves for growth but also increase resilience, because they are directly connected to solving real-world challenges.

This idea aligns closely with the Jobs to Be Done theory, which emphasizes that customers do not "buy" products; they "hire" them to solve problems. The difference is that the Success Point explicitly frames this in terms of value creation: Solving a customer's problem is not enough unless the customer recognizes and receives value in the process.

Figure 4.1 illustrates this intersection as a Venn diagram: customer–problem–value, with the Point of Success at the center.

Earlier, we touched on the challenge of identifying the customer. Now, we return to that theme, but in a broader and more strategic lens—not just who the customer is but how their problems connect to the value they get by getting that problem solved. This three-way equation—*customer +*

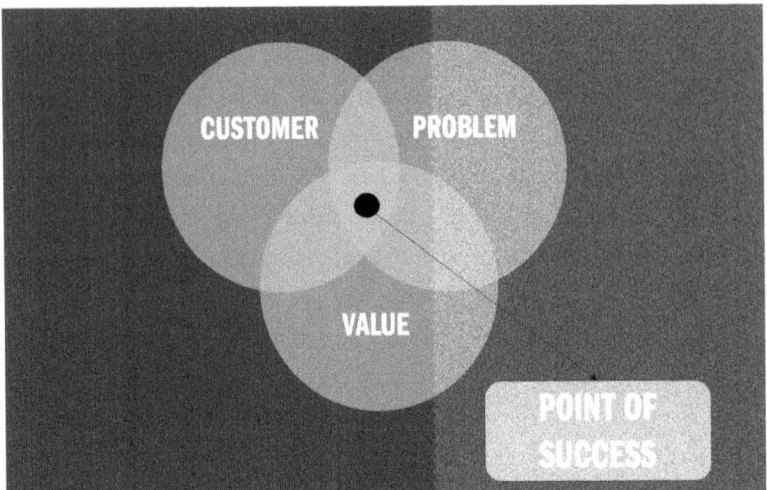

Figure 4.1 Success point. The intersection between customer, problem, and value

problem + value—is the foundation of the "point of success," the moment where real impact becomes possible.

Customer

In recent years, we have witnessed two parallel movements: the explosion of new technology companies and the reinvention of more traditional companies as they race to create digital products. Why this acceleration? Because, consciously or unconsciously, companies are discovering new problems that can be solved—problems that, until recently, were invisible or considered irrelevant.

As the saying goes, "We don't know what we don't know." My father often jokes: "If I go to the doctor, I might find out I'm ill. If I don't go, I stay healthy." Of course, reality is less comforting. The problem is there whether or not we look for it. In business, this ignorance used to be reinforced by limited technological capabilities. If there was no way to address a problem, it was simply ignored. Technology has changed that. With the rise of platforms like Uber, Netflix, and Amazon, consumers have realized there are better, faster, cheaper, or more convenient ways of solving needs they had long accepted as unsolvable. This recognition unlocks potential for innovation—and for disruption.

Take Uber as an example. Its success did not come from designing better cars, but from redefining the key problems: *mobility*, *pricing*, and *accessibility*. Consumers were not frustrated because of the car model they sat in—they were frustrated by high taxi prices, long waits, and the inconvenience of always needing their own vehicle. Uber provided a flexible, scalable solution. The customer did not "buy an app." They bought the ability to get from A to B much easily and quite affordable.

But Uber did more than solve problems for passengers. It also solved problems for drivers, who gained flexibility and direct access to customers outside of traditional taxi firms. In this sense, Uber is a platform business: It serves at least two distinct customer groups—the drivers and the passengers. And like any complex company, it also has internal customers: operations teams, digital teams, and others who rely on technology to make the system work.

This leads to a broader point: The customer is not only the one who pays. Customers are anyone whose needs, if unmet, can negatively impact performance.

Beyond the Obvious Customer

Consider a building materials company. At first glance, its customers are simply the construction firms who buy materials. Correct—but incomplete. Even within this external group, there are distinct profiles:

- Customers who purchase large volumes infrequently, focusing on discounts, contract terms, and distribution
- Customers who purchase small volumes frequently, prioritizing speed, low bureaucracy, and rapid delivery

From a digital transformation perspective, these profiles matter. Technology solutions must reflect their different problems. A "one-size-fits-all" solution risks failing both.

And those are just external customers. Inside the company, logistics operators, finance teams, and production staff also depend on digital solutions to work efficiently. If technology enables the end customer to order quickly but fails to support logistics with visibility over stock, the overall service collapses.

Restaurants provide another example. We naturally define the diner as the customer. Yet the cashier taking orders or the waiter serving tables is also a customer of the company's systems. If their tools are inadequate, the diner's experience suffers—and the diner never returns.

The Value Chain Perspective

A company is ultimately a value chain: a series of interconnected steps in which each piece contributes to generating value for the next. Ignoring customers at any point in that chain risks breaking the entire system.

This is why many companies invest heavily in User Experience groups for external products, but don't apply the same diligence to create similar products for internal customers. The result? Beautiful apps for consumers paired with clunky, frustrating internal tools. And when internal processes break down, external service inevitably deteriorates, so what's the point?

Rethinking Priorities

As I mentioned in an earlier chapter, it is common to hear people say: "I work for my manager," and often in leadership discussions one would say, that relationship is the key to keep talent motivated. However, while managers and organizations provide direction, the real answer is probably different: We all work for customers, in the sense of what we do and who gets the value of our work. They are the ones who ultimately determine whether our efforts succeed or fail.

Understanding this principle—that customers, internal and external, define success—reshapes priorities. It forces leaders to ask: *Whom do we serve? What problem are we solving for them? How do we ensure that solving it creates value?*

When companies are clear on who their customers really are, they are better positioned to identify the problems worth solving, and to design digital transformations that create real, lasting value.

Problem

Steve Jobs once said that companies should get close to their customers and observe the shortcuts and manual processes they use to overcome daily frustrations. These "workarounds" are often the best indicators of the true problem worth solving.

Yet, in many companies I've seen, this practice is rare. Problems are often defined by layers of intermediaries, many of whom lack field experience. It is more of an opinion exercise, and less of a true voice representing those needs. They interpret customer signals through spreadsheets, reports, and meetings—rather than direct observation. The result? Solutions designed for imagined problems, not real ones.

I've long admired Professor Clayton Christensen from Harvard Business School, who gave us the Jobs to Be Done theory. His milkshake example remains one of the clearest illustrations.

At first glance, a milkshake is a milkshake. But Christensen noticed that the reason for purchase changes everything. In the morning, commuters in the United States bought milkshakes because they needed something to occupy themselves during long traffic jams. The job wasn't "buy a drink" but "make a boring commute more tolerable." For this, a thicker shake worked best, because it lasted longer. In the afternoon, however, people wanted a quick treat during a short break. Now, the job was "satisfy a craving fast." A thick milkshake failed here—consumers needed something easier to drink.

The insight: The same product can solve different problems, depending on context. And those contexts define entirely different markets.

- In the morning, milkshakes compete not just with other milkshakes but with bananas, cereal bars, and lattes—anything that makes a commute manageable.
- In the afternoon, they compete with cookies, snacks, and sodas—things consumed quickly between tasks.

From this lens, we don't have one milkshake market. We have multiple markets, each defined by the problem being solved.

The Strategic Trap of "Solving the Wrong Problem"

This shift in thinking has profound implications for digital transformation. One of the biggest obstacles I see is twofold:

1. Companies fail to identify the core problem they are supposed to solve.
2. Even if they do, they struggle to test whether solving it will actually contribute to the company's long-term strategic goals.

Too often, technology projects start with a shopping list of requirements:

- "We need an app."
- "We need AI."
- "We need blockchain."

But requirements are not problems. Requirements are many times… solutions. And when companies chase technology for its own sake, they risk creating products that look sophisticated—but fail to solve what truly matters to their customers.

Twitter Versus Facebook: Solving Different Problems

Look at Facebook and Twitter. They are both "social networks." But they solved different problems when they first came out:

1. Twitter: Made to be like an SMS for the Web—short, to-the-point updates that are important. It made it easier to quickly share information, which was especially helpful for journalists, business leaders, and other people with a lot of ideas. Its worth comes from the discipline of being short.
2. Facebook: Made to be a digital profile wall where you can share your identity, photos, stories, and connections. It fixed the problem of keeping and growing relationships. Its worth comes from its richness and continuity.

This is why many people use both, but for very different reasons. You can't use one instead of the other. You have to say what's important in 140 characters on Twitter. You can share anything on Facebook without any limits.

What did you learn? Products that look the same on the outside may or may not work, depending on whether they are solving the right problem for the right customer.

Bringing It Back to Business Strategy

When companies embark on digital transformation, identifying the problem isn't enough. Leaders must ask:

- Does solving this problem move us closer to our vision?
- Does it connect with our FRAME pillars (business model, market, strategy, organization, processes)?
- Will solving this problem differentiate us in the market, or merely bring us to parity?

This reflection prevents organizations from investing years and millions into "fixes" that don't create real value.

Practical Case: The Materials Company

Imagine a building materials company. Two customers exist:

- Large contractors buying in bulk, infrequently
- Small builders buying small quantities, frequently

If the company assumes "the problem" is just "make buying easier," it might create a one-size-fits-all digital platform. But the problems are different:

- Large contractors care about bulk discounts, reliable logistics, and visibility of supply chains.
- Small builders care about speed, low bureaucracy, and quick pick-up.

A single, generic solution would fail both groups. But by starting with their problems, the company can design digital tools that are segment-specific—and therefore far more valuable. The question lies, however: Can the company tackle both? Are both fitting the vision set the by the company. By tackling both, can the company truly establish differentiators?

This may sound an easy answer, but it is not. It is fundamental to acknowledge that sometimes, we can't serve everyone, and choices are needed. Remember… its more often about what we cannot do. If we can address both, then we need to work around the two problems without compromising, as otherwise, at best bring us on pair, but not the true right to win.

Why Some Start-Ups Fail

I often tell start-up founders: "You didn't fail because you lacked talent. You failed because you built something you liked, not something people needed." A big risk, when we fall in love with our product, even though no one needs it. The market rewards problem-solvers, not hobbyists. When companies solve the right problem, they unlock a cycle of value:

- Solving a problem generates customer trust.
- Trust generates repeated business.
- Repeat business generates resources to solve more problems.

That cycle is the engine of sustainable digital transformation.

Value

When most people hear the word "value," they think of money right away. This is because value is something you get in exchange for a product, service, or effort. And yes, from a business point of view, value often does mean money, either directly or indirectly.

For instance, cutting down on the time it takes to finish a task can be seen as saving money.

- Lowering turnover costs can be done by making employees happier.
- Higher sales or fewer returns can show that the quality of the product has gone up.

It's understandable that this change into financial metrics is necessary for making decisions. But it can also be a problem.

I think that value should be thought of in a much broader way when it comes to digital transformation. Value is not just about money for employees or customers. It is measured by the results that are important to them.

Value can mean:

- Goodwill: feeling respected, heard, or supported
- Time: getting back hours that would have been lost to red tape
- Less frustration: making things easier instead of more complicated
- Quality: getting better at work or in life
- Opportunities: giving people the chance to sell, connect, or grow

In short, value is what a customer or user hopes to get out of using a product. And the most important test is whether that value is closely related to the problem that needs to be solved.

A lot of digital transformations fail here. It's surprisingly easy to lose focus and come up with elegant, high-tech solutions that look good on paper but don't really solve any problems. Something that looks "cool" but doesn't solve a real problem may get people excited at first, but it won't last.

That's why I say that value in isolation has no value.

Value only matters when:

1. It is given to a certain customer, whether they are inside or outside the company
2. A problem that is important to that customer

This is the main point of success: where the customer, the problem, and the value meet.

The Picture-Hanging Example

Think back to the simple case of hanging a picture on a wall. A drill creates a hole, but no one values the hole itself. The value comes from being able to hang the picture. The customer problem was "securely mount a picture," not "make a hole in the wall." The drill was just one way to achieve it.

If another tool solves that problem more easily, customers will abandon the drill—even if the drill is technically "better."

Value in Digital Transformation

When businesses go through digital transformation, they are basically redesigning their products and services for both outside markets and internal users so that customers can get the most out of their "points of success."

- For customers outside the company, this means products that meet their needs, fix their problems, and give them results that matter to them.
- For internal customers (employees and departments), it means systems and processes that make things easier, clearer, and help them do their jobs better.

When done right, digitalization is the process of systematically mapping customers to problems to value and then using technology to make those solutions bigger and better.

Value as Strategy

To sustain this, value must be linked to the vision of the company. Otherwise, transformation risks becoming fragmented:

- If your vision is to serve small retailers, don't invest in solving hypermarket problems.
- If your goal is speed and accessibility, don't focus all your energy on customization and complexity.

Strategic clarity is essential. Without it, companies risk pursuing "value" that excites in the short term but misaligns with long-term objectives.

The Bigger Picture

When companies approach transformation through this lens—customer, problem, value—they may not always create the next Twitter or Airbnb. But they will:

- Stay closer to their customers.
- Build solutions that matter.
- Anchor transformation in problems worth solving.
- Continuously focus on what generates real, enduring value.

That, ultimately, is how transformation becomes not just digital but successful.

The Customer Journey and the Value Chain

We looked at the parts of transformation in the last few chapters: markets, customers, problems, value, operations, and products. Each of these is very important on its own, but they don't stand alone. These parts need to work together as part of a single system for a digital transformation to work.

Starting with the customer's point of view is one of the best ways to make this integration happen. How do customers talk to the business? What do they do? How do those steps fit in with or not fit in with the company's own processes?

These are the two main ideas that come into play here:

- The Customer Journey is the path that customers take from first hearing about a company to their experience after they buy something. It shows how they see and interact with the company.
- The Value Chain is the order of tasks that happen inside the company that all work together to give the customer value.

Each approach gives us information on its own:

- The customer journey maps out expectations, touchpoints, and pain points.
- The value chain shows how things work inside the company, what they depend on, and how resources move around.

But when the two are put together, they really show their power. Companies can find gaps, misalignments, and chances for change by connecting the outside journey with the inside chain.

We will also talk about a third approach later in this chapter. This is a combined journey that brings together the customer's point of view and the company's value chain into one clear framework. This mixed view lets us see not only how customers go through their experience but also how the company's operations help (or hurt) each step of that experience.

In other words:

- The customer journey shows us what the customer goes through.
- The value chain tells us what the business does.
- The combined approach shows us how to manage both of them at the same time, interconnected to some of our approach (four blocks of transformation).

Value Chain

A value chain represents the set of activities performed by an organization from supplier relationships and production and sales cycles to the final distribution stage.

—Michael Porter[14]

Michael Porter's definition of the value chain remains one of the most influential concepts in strategy and management. At its core, the value chain describes how an organization transforms inputs into outputs

---

[14]Michael E. Porter, *Competitive Advantage: Creating and Sustaining Superior Performance* (Free Press, 1985), 33–61.

through a sequence of connected activities. From sourcing raw materials, through production and logistics, to sales and after-sales services—every activity either adds to or detracts from the final value delivered to the customer.

The value chain is not simply a process map. It is a strategic lens:

- It highlights how each activity contributes to competitive advantage.
- It reveals where costs are incurred and where differentiation can be created.
- It shows how external suppliers and internal functions interconnect to generate value.

Traditionally, Porter divided activities into primary activities (inbound logistics, operations, outbound logistics, marketing and sales, and service) and support activities (infrastructure, HR, technology, procurement). This distinction helps companies see that value creation is not only in the final product or service but also in everything that enables it.

Take the example of an e-commerce retailer:

- Inbound logistics involves receiving and managing stock from suppliers.
- Operations include managing the digital platform, product catalogs, and order systems.
- Outbound logistics is the fulfillment process: packaging, shipping, and delivery.
- Marketing and sales involve digital advertising, recommendation engines, and loyalty programs.
- Service includes customer support, returns handling, and ongoing engagement.

Alongside these, the support activities—such as technology infrastructure (servers, payment systems), HR (training customer service staff), and procurement (choosing logistics partners)—enable the entire system to function.

In the digital age, the value chain becomes even more critical. Why? Because technology has the potential to reconfigure activities, reduce friction, and even eliminate steps altogether. For example:

- AI-driven demand forecasting reduces the need for manual planning in inbound logistics.
- Automated chatbots transform customer service processes.
- Direct-to-consumer channels cut out intermediaries in distribution.

When companies fail in digital transformation, it is often because they implement technology in isolated activities without aligning the whole chain. Optimizing a single step (e.g., faster checkouts) does not guarantee transformation if upstream or downstream steps remain outdated (e.g., poor logistics or limited after-sales service).

For transformation to succeed, leaders must look at the entire value chain, mapping where value is added, where bottlenecks exist, and how digital can unlock new ways of creating value.

However, one of the limitations of Porter's original framework is that it was designed primarily with physical goods in mind. The activities of sourcing, manufacturing, transporting, and selling made perfect sense in 1985, but the digital economy has redefined the way value is created and distributed.

The digital economy[15]—understood as "the entrepreneurial process that generates digital value through socio-digital components that enable the acquisition, processing, distribution, and consumption of digital information"—requires us to rethink the traditional value chain.

People's buying habits have transformed and so have the demands on businesses to change how their chains work. For instance, a fashion store that used to sell through seasonal physical collections still can afford to ship more slowly and make things overseas, however, with e-commerce and fast fashion cycles, speed to market is very important.

---

[15]Jean-Michel Sahut, Luca Iandoli, and Frédéric Teulon, "The Age of Digital Entrepreneurship," *Small Business Economics* 56, no. 3 (2021): 1161, https://doi.org/10.1007/s11187-019-00260-8.

To stay competitive, production may need to be closer to consumers. Ads that used to work on billboards and TV must change to reach people who now find products through search engines, social media, and influencers. This means putting money into digital marketing, personalized content, and campaigns based on data.

It is obvious what this means: The modern value chain isn't just about being efficient; it is also about being flexible. Digital technologies that cross traditional boundaries make it possible for each link in the chain to quickly respond to changing customer needs.

The value chain is no longer fixed in this way. It has turned into a dynamic ecosystem where things like logistics, marketing, service, and even research and development are always changing to keep up with how people act. Mapping the value chain today for companies going through digital transformation means not only figuring out where value is made but also predicting where new value could come from in the future.

Customer Journey

The customer journey describes the experience a customer (or potential customer) has from the moment they first come into contact with a brand or product, through the process of purchase, and even into the stages of after-sales service and ongoing loyalty.[16]

This approach aims to map the stages a customer goes through while interacting with the company's channels, products, or services. It helps us understand:

- What behaviors we expect customers to demonstrate at each stage
- What questions or doubts they may have
- Which touchpoints (communication or interaction channels) are most suitable for keeping them engaged

Companies can come up with better plans to guide customers through each step of the journey by simply … imagining it. This will reduce friction and make the experience more meaningful.

---

[16]Bruce D. Temkin, *Mapping the Customer Journey*, Forrester Research report, February 5, 2010.

There are many different approaches, and often times companies customize their own, but a common way to break down the customer journey is into five main steps:

- Awareness: The customer realizes they have a need or a problem and finds out about your business. At this point, marketing, brand awareness, and building a good reputation are all important.
- Consideration: The customer starts to compare their options, weigh their options, and figure out which ones best meet their needs. In this case, product information, content marketing, and trustworthiness are very important.
- Buying (Decision): When the customer decides to buy your product or service. Things like how easy it is to buy, how much you can trust the company, how clear the prices are, and how good the user experience are very important.
- Service (Onboarding/Support): After the sale, the focus moves to how well the product or service works. Customer service, technical support, and onboarding all play a big role in how happy the customer is at this point.
- Expanding loyalty: A happy customer might buy more, upgrade, or even become a brand ambassador. This stage gets stronger with loyalty programs, ongoing engagement, and interactions that add value.

These five phases are a standard reference model, but it's important to remember that the journey isn't always straight. Customers can skip steps, go back, or repeat phases based on what they need and what's going on. Also, in digital settings, journeys are often multichannel or omnichannel, and nonsequential, which means that customers can talk to your brand at any time on social media, websites, in stores, or even through word of mouth.

Awareness

The awareness phase marks the beginning of the customer journey, situated in the presales stage. At this point, the customer is not yet making a purchase decision; rather, they are realizing or acknowledging a problem, need, or desire.

This stage is less about identifying specific platforms (social media, websites, advertising, etc.) and more about understanding the behaviors and triggers that bring a potential customer into contact with the company, product, or brand. For example, a customer may recognize a recurring frustration, encounter a recommendation from a peer, or notice a gap between their expectations and the current solutions available.

The essential objective of this stage is not to "sell" immediately, but to make the problem visible and position the company as a potential enabler of its resolution. When mapped correctly, awareness provides insights into:

- How customers perceive the existence of a problem
- What signals or behaviors indicate this recognition
- What types of interactions (searching, browsing, listening, asking, testing) typically occur before they even consider alternatives

In other words, awareness is the stage where the customer starts a journey not because of the company's push but because of their own pull—the recognition that there is something missing that might require action.

Consideration

The consideration phase is the next step after the customer realizes, they have a problem or need. In this phase, they actively look for possible solutions. The problem has already become part of you at this point; the question now is how to deal with it.

When you move into a new house, you have to fix the frames on the wall. This makes you open to looking for solutions, like buying a drilling machine, using adhesive hooks, or hiring a handyman. The customer is now open to different ways to get the job done.

The consideration phase is when you gather information by looking into solutions, reading reviews, and trying out different options.

- Comparing and judging: looking at the pros and cons of each option, including their features, costs, and how easy they are to use
- Willingness to be influenced: Customers are open to communication that points out differences, value propositions, or unique benefits.

This is a very important time for companies to compete. Customers are not yet fully committed but are shaping preferences. To be successful, you need to be clear, relevant, and trustworthy. Knowing what factors affect decision making, like price, usability, reputation, convenience, or sustainability, and choosing the right channels for the right people can often make the difference between getting the sale or not.

To put it simply, consideration is the stage of possibility. The customer is no longer just passively looking at options; they are actively seeking them, and the company's job is to help them see its solution as the best one.

Buying

The buying phase is the most important time for the customer to pick a solution and finish the deal. If this stage isn't easy, trustworthy, and seamless, all the money spent on raising awareness and getting people to think about it could be wasted.

People may make a purchase based on their feelings or their logic, or a mix of the two. The important thing is that the company makes it easy for the customer to do what they want when they are ready. The risk of abandonment goes up a lot if the process is slow, unclear, or unsafe.

This is when multichannel and omnichannel strategies become very important. Customers expect the same level of service whether they are shopping in a store, on a website, through a mobile app, or even on social media. The experience should give:

- Ease: little friction, easy-to-use design, and quick checkout
- Trust: clear information, prices that are easy to understand, and safe payments
- Flexibility: you can choose from different ways to buy, have it delivered, or return it

The company's job at this point is to get rid of obstacles. Awareness and consideration are about getting people to buy something, but buying is about doing it without any problems. Success is less about impressing the customer and more about helping them follow through on their decision with confidence and on their own terms.

In short, if buying seems harder than thinking about it, the sale is lost.

Service

How many of us haven't been angry after calling the helpline of a phone company, an insurance company, or any other service provider? Getting in touch with support centers is almost always necessary for long-lasting consumer goods. These moments can determine if the relationship with the customer gets better over time or falls apart completely.

A common mistake is to think of service as just a cost center. In reality, it drives value. After a customer buying something, every interaction with them is a chance to either:

- Turn frustration into loyalty by quickly and kindly fixing problems, or
- Break trust and lose the customer for good.

Customers are often already stressed when they ask for help. They don't expect perfection; they just want you to be honest about wanting to fix the problem. If the process is bureaucratic, slow, or dismissive, they will not only be angry with the support experience but also with the product itself, even if the product is technically sound.

The main point is that customers can't separate the quality of a product from the quality of the service. Companies that don't spend enough on support are betting that their products will work so well that they won't need support. This is not a long-term approach, and though it might work in some very specific situations, it may eventually backfire.

Proactivity, or anticipating problems before the customer has to deal with them, is often a part of modern service excellence.

- Self-service and freedom: giving customers the tools they need to solve problems on their own, when it's convenient for them
- Human empathy where it counts: making sure that when you need to talk to someone in person, it doesn't feel like a business transaction

Building a call center the size of a Premier League stadium is not what great service is all about. It's about knowing what customers want in terms of independence, speed, and empathy, and then making service touchpoints that meet those needs.

In the end, service isn't a way to protect yourself; it's a way to build relationships, keep customers from leaving, and even make new sales.

Expanding Loyalty

We should never take for granted the privilege of having a loyal customer. Being contractually tied to a brand for 24 months does not mean you are loyal to it. Real loyalty is something you choose to do, feel, and have with someone else. When a customer chooses to stay connected to a product or brand even though there are other options that are easier to get.

This kind of attachment often goes beyond what makes sense. The classic example of Apple is that many people openly say they can't imagine giving up their iPhone for a Samsung phone (or the other way around). They can switch if they want to, but the emotional bond keeps them from doing so. This is what makes loyalty different from just keeping customers.

Companies that know how to create loyalty can use this process to build stronger ties with their customers. Once more, Apple is a clear example. Someone who owns an iPhone is much more likely to buy an iPad, sign up for iTunes, or switch to MacOS. Loyalty opens the door to an ecosystem where each product makes the others more valuable.

The effects on digital transformation are huge:

- A loyal customer is less likely to care about price, more likely to forgive mistakes, and more willing to try new things.
- Loyalty increases value: A happy customer is not only more likely to buy from you again but may also become an advocate and tell their friends, family, or coworkers about your brand.
- Loyalty speeds up the adoption of new ideas: Customers who trust the brand are more likely to try new products, even in categories that haven't been tested yet.

The main goal of any customer journey design should be to make it possible for this kind of loyalty to grow and spread. Companies can go from short-term business relationships with their customers to long-term partnerships with them at this point, which will help them grow in a sustainable way.

Final Thoughts

The customer journey approach is a popular way to plan marketing and customer acquisition strategies because it helps businesses figure out what will happen at each step and how to change or use behavior. This method is even more useful now that digital products are being made, mostly because tech-based interactions are more predictable.

As I said before, personas are a good addition to this method. Customer journey maps show the steps, but personas make those steps real by adding details. It can be hard to personalize things when you segment them at too high a level. Personas, on the other hand, make it easier to plan behaviors and interactions that are expected. For example, "John, who likes surfing, eats healthy, and doesn't like technology very much" is much easier to analyze and plan for than a group of people like "customers in northern Portugal who like the beach." The clearer the journey definition gets, the more accurate the profile is.

This kind of method isn't just for big companies; it works for small ones too. For example, think about a restaurant. It's important to remember that just because a reservation service or personalized ordering system exists, customers won't just show up. A great product is useless if no one knows about it. Similarly, great food and service that can't handle orders is just as useless as great marketing that can't deliver. For long-term growth, every step of the customer journey is important, and happy customers are the result of making sure all of those steps work together well.

It is also important to remember that the customer journey can be used for internal customers. But it should be changed and made easier to understand because internal dynamics are different. Internal customers don't usually go through separate awareness or consideration phases. These phases do exist, but the company's strategy shapes them. Still, mapping internal journeys can help find problems, make things run more smoothly, and make sure that internal processes don't hurt customer satisfaction.

In the end, whether it's external or internal, designing a customer journey is about making a clear and predictable path where each step adds value, makes things easier, and creates an environment where loyalty can grow.

Customer and the Value Journey

The two methodologies we just discussed—the customer journey and the value chain—are both very powerful in helping us understand how a company should work end-to-end, and how a customer interacts with a product or service.

Yet, when used separately, they also present a limitation. Analyzing a customer's experience without connecting it to what happens "behind the curtain" (the operations, logistics, or technology that support each step) risks leading to fragmented solutions. On the other hand, looking only at the value chain without the customer's lens makes companies fall into the trap of efficiency without relevance.

That is why I combined (with some flavors) what I call the Customer and Value Journey—a combined view that overlays the customer journey with the company's value blocks. By doing this, we create a single view that forces us to see both sides: the experience the customer expects, and the operations required to deliver it.

This approach also integrates the four blocks of the digital transformation that I introduced earlier in the book. Together, they form a practical tool that helps leaders and teams design digital transformation in a way that is strategic, customer-centric, and operationally grounded.

The Two Dimensions

The methodology crosses two well-defined dimensions:

1. Customer Journey Phases—the six steps customers go through when interacting with a company:
   - Awareness—realizing the problem
   - Effective Interest—deciding they want to solve it
   - Sales Support—engaging with the company to buy
   - Execution—the process of delivery, use, or execution
   - Customer Care—ongoing support, service, relationship
   - After-Sales—loyalty, expansion, and repurchase
2. Value Blocks of Digital Transformation—the four blocks that represent the company's internal capacity to deliver:
   - External Positioning—marketing, communication, reputation, branding
   - Product—the actual product or service offered
   - Product Support Operations—logistics, purchasing, support functions
   - Technology—the systems and digital capabilities enabling everything

The View

When we combine these two dimensions, we create a matrix where each customer phase intersects with the company's value blocks. This makes it possible to ask very concrete questions:

- What is the customer expectation at this step?
- Which value block(s) need to act, and how?
- How do we ensure alignment between external perception and internal delivery?

Here's how the combined model looks in table form:

Customer Journey	External Positioning (Brand and Market)	Product (Core Offer)	Product Support Operations (Logistics, Service, Processes)	Technology (Digital Enablers)
1. Awareness	Create visibility; campaigns; brand mission; show problem relevance	N/A at this stage	N/A	Data analytics to identify prospects; SEO, social targeting
2. Effective Interest	Demonstrate competitive advantage; storytelling	Adapt features to resonate with personas	N/A	CRM, personalization engines, content delivery
3. Sales Support	Clear, transparent communication; trust-building	Product clarity (composition, benefits)	Sales process support, logistics integration	E-commerce, omnichannel platforms
4. Execution	Reinforce trust (on-time delivery, ethical branding)	Product must deliver as promised	Production, logistics, fulfillment	ERP integration, order-to-delivery systems
5. Customer Care	Relationship building; ongoing trust	Durable/ reliable product	Customer support, FAQs, service models	Self-service platforms, AI chatbots, knowledge base
6. After-Sales	Loyalty campaigns, referrals, subscriptions	Product extensions, upsells	Return processes, repurchase support	Data-driven campaigns, loyalty platforms

This table makes it explicit: Every phase of the customer journey is tied to one or more value blocks. No phase is "just marketing" or "just operations." It is always an integrated experience.

Of course, this table is highly simplified, and it is designed to provide a view of the approach, and not an exhaustive description. You may wonder where you find the value chain. If you look carefully, it is spread through multiple areas of the matrix, with very high incidence in the Product Support (Operations), where we connect the process behind the channels.

Practical Case: Natural Cleaning

Let's illustrate with a small company: Natural Cleaning, a 40-person business that produces eco-friendly cleaning products.

Vision: "To become the benchmark brand for natural cleaning, with a strong presence in digital commerce and guaranteed delivery in under 24 hours."

Two strategic premises emerge:

- Digital-first commerce
- Distribution chain ready for 24-hour delivery

Personas defined: Fernando and Helena, an environmentally conscious couple in their 30s/40s, vegan, active recyclers, committed to reducing environmental impact.

Now, applying the combined Customer and Value Journey:

- Awareness and External Positioning—Instagram campaigns and storytelling emphasizing the environmental mission. Appeal to their values: "a clean home without harming the planet."
- Effective Interest and Technology—personalized digital campaigns, CRM data, and tailored content to make Fernando and Helena feel the product fits their lifestyle.
- Sales Support and Operations—a seamless e-commerce platform that explains ingredients clearly, offers quick purchase, and en ables expert chat for reassurance.
- Execution and Product/Operations/Technology—ensure the product quality speaks for itself. Guarantee delivery within 24 hours through logistics partners, enabled by tech integration between factory and courier.
- Customer Care and Technology/Operations—provide independence through self-service FAQs and eco-content, minimizing costly service calls while strengthening the brand's environmental credibility.
- After-Sales and Loyalty—targeted campaigns, subscriptions for recurring deliveries, and creative engagement through digital loyalty platforms

Why It Matters

By combining customer journey, value chain, and the four blocks of transformation, we avoid isolated thinking. Each customer interaction is directly tied to the internal processes that sustain it. This creates a 360-degree view where:

- The customer sees relevance at every touchpoint.
- The company sees efficiency in how it allocates resources.
- Technology is treated as a core enabler, not an afterthought.

This view does not replace strategy—it builds on it. It assumes a clear vision and personas have been defined. But once those foundations are in place, the Customer and Value Journey ensures that transformation is aligned, scalable, and customer centric.

And with this foundation, we are ready to move to the next step: strategies for digital transformation.

PART 3

How to Make the Right Decisions

Turning Ambition into Direction, and Direction into Practical Choices

Diagnosis reveals what must change; this part is about choosing how it will. We move from understanding to decision—clarifying direction, focus, and what success must look like.

In the previous chapters, we explored the company from different perspectives: its markets, its customers, the problems they face, and how the organization can design products and operations to truly meet their needs. But all this analysis becomes almost meaningless if the company does not build the skills and strategies necessary to act on it.

In the earlier chapters of this book, I emphasized the importance of looking at SWOT. That exercise was not meant as a theoretical warm-up; it was a key step toward action. A digital transformation only becomes real when those insights are converted into strategies, so we maximize strengths, minimize weaknesses, seize opportunities, and mitigate threats.

This chapter is about that translation. We now turn to the strategic options available to organizations seeking digital transformation. These strategies are not exhaustive—no book could possibly cover every variation across industries—but they represent a set of approaches I have seen work in practice. They are not prescriptive "templates," instead, think of it as strategic levers or options a leadership team can choose, combine, or adapt to fit its context in different phases of the exercise.

The Dilemma of Transforming While Performing

Start-ups have the privilege of the blank page. They can define a bold vision without the weight of legacy systems, ingrained culture, or historical customers. They can imagine an entirely new market, unburdened by tradition.

Most established companies, however, do not have this luxury. They must transform while performing: adapt their models, products, and processes without halting the day-to-day operations that keep them alive. This is where the real complexity of digital transformation lies.

Several critical questions arise:

- Should we focus on efficiency and digitalize existing operations?
- Should we target new market segments?
- Should we reinvent the business model entirely to compete with digital-first entrants?

The answers are not theoretical. They require trade-offs, courage, and above all, clarity of vision.

The Challenge of Resistance

One of the greatest obstacles is resistance to changing the business model itself. For many companies, the business model is part of their identity. To alter it feels like a betrayal of their history.

And yet, can they avoid it? The evidence says no. McKinsey's[17] analysis of the pandemic showed that digital adoption accelerated by a decade's worth of growth in a matter of months. Consumer habits shifted almost overnight, from physical stores to digital platforms. I experienced it myself: In 2020 and 2021, I almost stopped going to physical shops. I even bought my car via Bynco, a fully digital platform. What changed? Not the car—the process.

---

[17]"Fifty-Five: The Quickenung," *McKinsey Quarterly*, https://www.mckinsey.com/business-functions/strategy-and-corporate-finance/our-insights/five-fifty-the-quickening.

Bynco realized that the inconvenience of purchasing the car was the issue that needed to be resolved, not the car itself. The customer journey was redefined by them. The same lesson holds true for all industries: Customers frequently still desire the same product, but it is presented in a different way.

In this setting, resistance to change is not only dangerous but existential. Businesses that put off adapting fall behind their quicker, more agile rivals. The Blockbuster and Netflix story is a cautionary tale, not a corny one.

When to Modify a Business Model

Not every change necessitates a business model revolution. In certain cases, such as when switching from physical to digital sales channels, it is sufficient to modify operations.

However, a true business model transformation occurs when the profit formula, sales mechanisms, or customer interaction models undergo fundamental changes.

Think about logistics. Large operators prospered for decades by transferring risks to clients, having long contracts, and having high volumes. However, technology-driven start-ups have brought logistics-as-a-service, which are subscription-style business models with no long-term commitments where customers pay for each shipment. The advantages of incumbents are already being undermined by this change, which was led by Amazon's fulfillment services.

It takes time to adjust to this new reality. Contracts, sales, pricing, operations, and technology—the very foundation of the business model—are all altered.

Technology's Strategic Role

Technology was viewed as infrastructure for many years, including websites, CRMs, and ERPs. It serves as the strategic foundation of business today. Businesses that base their business models heavily on technology are nearly always the ones that cause disruption.

Technology leaders will, in my opinion, increasingly hold senior executive positions in a variety of industries, not just tech companies. Why? Because strategy now requires an understanding of digital platforms, consumer expectations, and the economics of automation.

Regardless of your industry, Amazon, Netflix, and Uber have set the standard for customer expectations in our world. Leaders who comprehend the reasoning behind those models are necessary to compete in this environment.

Digital Transformation: 10 Strategic Levers

In light of this, let's examine 10 tactics and resources that can assist businesses in planning their digital transformation. They are all levers that can be pulled to implement change, align vision, and increase capabilities.

I have organized it in three major groups:

- Foundation: The basics that ultimately shall exist in any organization one way or another
- Strategic Choices: How to leverage the Four-Floor Model to define the right initiatives that successfully deliver a strategy
- Disruption: While the concept of disruption can vary, these are levers that may imply fundamental changes across your business model, market, strategy, organization or processes.

1. **Set the foundations to transform**
   a. Vision First, Everything Else Second.
      Transformation is impossible without a compelling vision. To bring employees together and draw in customers, a business needs a clear and motivating north star. The reason for the transformation is made clear by vision; everything else falls into place.
   b. Business Strategy
      Without a plan, a vision is just a dream. As one of the five pillars, we go over strategy again (FRAME). Here, we take a closer look at how to match operations, products, and markets with long-term objectives.

2. **The Four-Floor Model**

   I created a useful tool that starts with a strategic vision statement and progresses through success criteria, challenges, and solutions. This model guarantees that transformation stays grounded by transforming the vision into operational actions.

3. **The disruption through technology**

   a. The Digital Service Economy

      What's the point of reinventing the wheel? Numerous features are already available as digital services, such as cloud infrastructure, logistics-as-a-service, and payment platforms. Sometimes integrating into preexisting ecosystems can bring about transformation without the need for construction.

   b. Silent Disruption and Digital Twins

      Digital versions of physical companies are subtly changing markets. Digital twins are revolutionizing operations and customer engagement in a variety of industries, including health care and real estate. Businesses need to foresee these changes before they become disastrous.

   c. The Digital Shortcut to Globalization

      Geographical barriers have been eliminated by digital. Customers in Tokyo or New York can now be reached by a small store in Lisbon. Globalization is now a structural fact rather than an option. This wider competitive landscape must be taken into consideration in strategy.

   d. Digital Commerce

      This is the front line of change for many. Online sales may start out as "just another channel," but they alter marketing, logistics, and operations. Digital commerce is a total redesign of value delivery, not just a website.

   e. The Strategic Impacts of Generative AI

      Generative AI creates new content, designs, and ideas, offering strategic value in innovation, customer engagement, decisions, and operations. From small shops to global firms, it enables scale and efficiency. Risks include bias, errors, and sameness. True advantage comes when leaders combine AI's power with human empathy, trust, and judgment.

f. Ten Tips for Getting Technology Right
    Technology is not about chasing trends but enabling strat-
    egy. This chapter presents my 10 tips for smarter technology
    choices: focus on customer value, build only what differentiates,
    keep systems simple, secure, and adaptable, harness data, auto-
    mation, and AI responsibly. The right decisions turn technology
    into growth, not a burden.

g. Hypothesis-Driven Strategy
    We are not able to foresee everything. Strategy must be based
    on fast-testable hypotheses in uncertain markets. Learn quickly
    and adapt quickly. Businesses can adapt without being para-
    lyzed by this experimental mindset.

Final Thoughts

Each business must determine which combination best suits its capabilities, culture, and vision.

Technology is not what digital transformation is all about. At a
rate never seen before, it is adjusting to consumers and markets. Direction comes from vision. Alignment is provided by strategy. Leaders are
equipped to take action by levers such as the digital service economy, the
Four Floors, and hypothesis-driven approaches.

However, none of it is possible without the true intent to change, the
desire to challenge what we know, welcome unknowns, and rethink the
company's future and possibilities.

CHAPTER 5

Set the Foundations to Transform

The base of every change is what makes it work or not. If the company doesn't know what it wants to do and why, new technologies, processes, or structures don't mean much. Too many companies start their digital journeys with action plans before they know what they want to achieve. This is because they confuse activity with direction. But having a vision is not optional. It is the first test of readiness and the thing that holds all talks about strategy, execution, and impact together.

You have to believe in change. People prefer things that are clear over things that are complicated. When leaders share a vision that is clear, believable, and emotionally grounded, it brings teams together and gives stakeholders confidence. But when the story isn't clear, the change falls apart because it's not clear. A good vision doesn't just tell people what the future will be like; it gives them a reason to make it happen.

This chapter talks about how to build that base. It starts with the art of telling stories, which is the elevator pitch that sums up your purpose and value in a few strong sentences. You'll learn how this skill helps you connect with both customers and employees, and how getting everyone on board is the first step to going digital. We'll look at real-life examples to see how leaders can make technology useful for their teams and how vision can be used as a design tool instead of just a slogan.

After that, we'll talk about strategy, which is how to turn a vision into clear choices. And last but not least, we'll talk about how to measure strategic success not with vanity metrics, but with real indicators that show progress and maturity.

Setting the foundations means putting together three important parts: vision, strategy, and measurement. Vision tells us why we are moving. Strategy tells us how to move. Measurement makes sure that we are really moving. If you don't have all three, change is just noise. It becomes intent with them—a disciplined path from belief to action, from ambition to success.

Vision First

We have two minutes and two sentences. How do we convince anyone that we have a product that gives them the value they are looking for?

In previous chapters, we touched lightly on vision. Here, we'll go deeper—because without vision, no digital transformation strategy can stand.

The Story of a Frozen Pitch

Some time ago, during strategic planning for one of the products in the company where I was managing director, we reached an impasse. One of our product managers was explaining the vision for a customer interaction platform, including digital commerce. Technically, everything made sense. But emotionally, it was uninspiring.

After a few back-and-forth, I asked her: "Imagine you have a one-time chance to meet the CEO. You need €1 million in investment. You have two minutes. How do you sell the vision for this product?"

For a moment she froze. Then, after reflecting, she said:

> We have physical account managers who spend the same amount of time with a large client as with a small one. The only way to scale our business is to ensure they focus on the big clients, while smaller ones get the same quality at a lower cost. That solution is the digital account manager—a digital replica of our physical account manager. If our company wants to be digital, that's where the million should go.

It didn't matter whether her pitch was perfect. What mattered was that she could articulate a clear, compelling vision that I understood and believed in. From that moment, we had something to work on.

The Elevator Pitch Mindset

What I asked of my product manager is often called an elevator pitch: a concise, high-impact story that convinces leaders, customers, or employees in seconds.

Throughout my career, I've used this test constantly. Too often, people respond with long, boring answers, buried in detail. It's human nature: We focus on details because they give us comfort and control. But the reality is that we rarely have more than a few moments to gain someone's attention.

No digital transformation succeeds without the support of influencers/ambassadors inside the company, employees on the ground, or customers outside. Designing a message that can attract this support is fundamental.

Think about the logic of teleshopping ads. They identify a relatable problem, dramatize its impact, and position their product as the obvious solution. Fifteen to thirty seconds, and the consumer is ready to buy. The Super Bowl half-time ads take this logic to the extreme with millions of potential customers, and a tiny window to capture attention and create urgency.

What about the *Shark Tank*. Entrepreneurs have minutes to sell their idea to investors. Sometimes you see brilliant products destroyed by poor communication. Other times, average products win big because the story resonates. The lesson is simple: Vision needs to be told clearly and inspiring, not just thought well defined.

Many things can go wrong of course:

- A product with limited growth potential
- A good product aimed at the wrong customer
- A great idea poorly executed
- An inability to articulate what value is created and why it matters

A strong pitch does not guarantee success, but a weak one definitely is likely to guarantee failure.

Where Vision Becomes Practical

Skeptics sometimes ask: "Is the elevator pitch really useful beyond sales?" My answer: Absolutely. It is as much a tool for designing vision as it is for selling it.

By forcing leaders to articulate the essence of their product or strategy in 30 to 60 seconds, it makes vision tangible and testable. It shows whether the message is clear enough, and whether it carries emotional weight.

In digital transformation, I see two contexts where this discipline is especially powerful:

1. Designing products for end customers. If the product vision cannot be explained simply, it will likely fail to resonate in the market.
2. Implementing new technologies internally. Employees must understand why the technology matters. If they don't "buy" the vision, adoption will stall.

Further down in the later chapters, we will talk about a model to transform behaviors, and how one of the key phases is the "intention," and how we create intentionality toward change. This elevator pitch can play a key role in generating that intention, when it leads to an emotional buy-in.

Ultimately, vision is not a "nice to have." It is the first filter through which every strategy, product, and initiative must pass. Without vision, companies drown in detail, lose alignment, and waste resources. With vision, they gain clarity, momentum, and belief.

Digital transformation is complicated. But if you cannot explain why it matters—in two sentences, in two minutes—you've already lost before the game even begun.

From Pitch to Product: Designing with Vision

First, we don't create an elevator pitch in isolation. In the context of digital transformation, the pitch is part of a broader sales and product design process. The short, telesales-style message is "just" one component, but it only works if it is anchored in a marketing plan and, above all, in a compelling product vision.

The value of the elevator pitch in external sales is not about finding the right slogan for an advertisement. It is about discipline in design. As we discussed earlier, the triangle of customer, problem, and value defines the point of success. The elevator pitch is a way of testing whether we can articulate that point of success in a way that makes sense, emotionally and strategically.

An elevator pitch is not the vision itself. It is the representation of that vision. A good pitch forces us to answer: *Have we really defined the problem? Do we know who the customer is? Can we show the value we create in one or two sentences?*

Used this way, an elevator pitch can help at multiple stages:

- Marketing campaigns—ensuring the message connects with the right audience
- Investor relations—convincing external stakeholders to fund the journey
- Internal alignment—securing management support and motivating colleagues

Vision Before Features

The real test of a product vision comes before a single feature is built. Too often, product teams obsess over functionalities rather than value. A strong elevator pitch reverses that, as it forces them to start with the customer and the problem and only then imagine features that could bring the vision to life.

Amazon offers a fascinating model here, the PRFAQ (Press Release, Frequently Asked Questions). Teams are asked to write a press release for the day of launch, before development even begins. The press release, though fictitious, forces the team to articulate what the company wants customers to know and feel about the product. No features, no technical details, just the essence of vision and value.

The second element, the FAQ, is equally powerful. Teams must anticipate the toughest questions customers, employees, and investors might ask: "Why should I switch?" "How is this different from the competition?" "What problem does it really solve?" This exercise forces a shift in perspective: from the producer's excitement over features to the customer's expectations of outcomes.

Together, PR and FAQ form a compass document that guides development. They anchor teams to vision and value instead of letting them drift into the comfort zone of incremental features.

Practical Case: Real Time Cleaning

Consider Real Time Cleaning, a medium-sized company with 120 employees, specializing in industrial cleaning services. The company has been losing market share: Larger clients prefer global operators, while smaller and midsize businesses feel overlooked. Leaders faced a choice: continue chasing large contracts they could never win or redesign their offer to fit the underserved segment of smaller, more flexible clients. They chose the latter.

They drafted a vision statement:

Real Time Cleaning wants to make industrial cleaning as simple as ordering food online. Any customer can find, book, and enjoy a spotless factory floor in no time at all. We're not just easy to book; we're the best at what we do.

Breaking it down:

- Customer perspective: small/medium companies without fixed schedules or big budgets
- Problem: lack of access to flexible, high-quality cleaning services
- Value: easy online booking, professional quality, and flexibility without large contracts

The vision is simple, clear, and emotionally compelling. Yet, to realize it, the company would need deep changes across its operations, technology, and external positioning. The elevator pitch here is not the end, but the starting line—a narrative to inspire change and direct investment.

From Story to Structure

Whether through a 30-second pitch, a PRFAQ, or a simple vision statement, the principle remains: Test the story before you test the product. If you cannot convince investors, leaders, or colleagues that your product matters, the odds of convincing customers are slim.

In a later chapter, we will look at the Four-Floor Model, a tool that guides you from vision to execution, bridging the story we tell with the initiatives we need.

Winning Internal Customers: Selling Technology Inside

When companies talk about digital transformation, they often focus on external customers, the ones who buy, subscribe, and generate revenue. However, as we discussed before, there is another group just as critical to success: internal customers. These are the employees who must use the systems, tools, and technologies that keep the company running.

Here lies the paradox: Unlike external customers, employees don't *choose* whether to buy or not. They are told, "Here is the system, now use it." But human beings don't work that way. Agreement does not equal intention; acceptance does not equal adoption. If employees don't understand the value of the technology, or if they don't want to use it, they will either misuse it, avoid it, or simply go through the motions without maximizing its potential. The result is likely to be increase in errors, process breakdowns, rising support tickets, and the return on investment falling short.

This is where an internal elevator pitch could play an interesting role. Just as you would never launch a new product without convincing customers of its benefits, you should never roll out new technology internally without first convincing your employees of the value it brings to them. Not only tell them but rather generate intention.

If we return to the customer–problem–value triangle, employees are not fundamentally different from paying customers:

- They have a perspective (their daily work, frustrations, and pressures).
- They experience problems (manual work, bottlenecks, errors, delays).
- They receive value if those problems are solved (time saved, recognition earned, less stress).

What often fails is the *message*. Too often, technology rollouts are framed as obligations, "this is the new system," rather than opportunities.

In other cases, the framing is just so complex that gets lost. The elevator pitch can serve as the bridge: a simple, emotionally compelling message that translates the system's value into the employee's language. Any transformation can consist of a set of elevator pitches for different components, and each should be sellable on its own.

Practical Case: Lightening Furniture

Consider Lightening Furniture, a 60-person company producing customized furniture with home delivery. Competing in a market dominated by IKEA, their edge lies in production speed.

To be competitive, they need a warehouse management system (WMS) to accelerate material handling. A vendor develops the system, but convincing the warehouse staff is the real challenge. These employees feel constant pressure: Delays in production are blamed on them, even when the real problem is lack of support.

So, the company designs an internal elevator pitch:

Without this warehouse, there is no furniture. Without furniture, there is no company. Our customers need production speed, and you are the solution to make that possible. This new logistics system will help you deliver faster, avoid delays, and be recognized for the value you create—not blamed for the problems you can't control.

- Customer perspective: warehouse staff who feel under pressure and undervalued
- Problem: delays in material handling create stress and damage reputation.
- Value: the system empowers them to deliver faster, gain recognition, and reduce blame.

This reframes the technology as a tool for *their success*, not just the company's.

Why Culture Shapes the Pitch

Every company has its own culture, and the way you craft an internal pitch must reflect it. In some companies, employees respond to recognition and pride; in others, they want independence and efficiency. The structure is always the same—simple message, focus on the problem solved, and clarity on value delivered—but the details must align with the expectations of each group. If one works for adidas versus working for IBM, there is a likelihood to apply different analogies, difference references, and so on. Make it relatable to content that are meaningful within that organization. Don't invent value. Highlight the aspects of value that matter most to that audience.

Adoption Is Change Management

Internal adoption is not just a technical project. It is change management. The elevator pitch is one of the most underused tools in this domain as it is way to convince employees that technology is here to make them stronger, not to threaten their jobs.

When companies fail to articulate this message, they create passive resistance, with employees complying, but not truly committing, resulting in underutilized systems, frustrated users, and wasted investment. When companies succeed, they transform internal customers into advocates, spreading adoption and reinforcing culture.

Think of any technology you are implementing right now. Ask yourself:

- Who are the internal customers?
- What problem are they facing?
- What value will they get from using this tool?

Then, write an elevator pitch of no more than three or four lines that speaks directly to them. Test it with colleagues. Refine it until it resonates.

Digital transformation is not just about systems but about people. Convince the inside first, and the outside will follow.

Business Strategy

You have to realize that technology is not a side component of business strategy—it is an integral part of it. Thinking of technology as "just" the IT department can jeopardize the entire business over time.

Strategy is one of those words that everyone uses, but few truly crack it. There is corporate strategy, financial strategy, human resources strategy, product strategy, marketing strategy—the list never stops growing. But above all of these sits the company strategy—the main, driving strategy. This is the one that defines what the company as a whole intends to do, and how it will get there.

All other strategies—whether HR, product, commercial, or technology—must flow from this central strategy, and when this doesn't happen, one of the basic principles of strategic design is broken. There can only be *one strategy*, which then cascades into different elements. Think of it as a tree: The corporate strategy is the trunk, and every substrategy is a branch that grows out of it. If branches grow in different directions without connection to the trunk, the tree eventually collapses.

Objectives Versus Strategy

One common confusion is between objectives and strategy. Saying, "We want to grow 10 percent per year" is not a strategy; it's an objective. Strategy should answer the *why* and the *how*, highlighting the narrative and the strategic choices. Objectives are the measurable outcomes that tell us whether the strategy is succeeding.

Take this practical case:

- Objective: Grow 10 percent in sales this year.
- Strategy (oversimplified): Expand into new digital marketplaces and leverage customer data to personalize offers, simplify checkout experience, increasing attraction, conversion rates and retention.

When a company embarks on digital transformation, it must ask the hard question: *Why?* "Because everyone else is doing it," "because we need it," "because that's how we grow" is not a strategy. At best, is an honest answer. The real answer, however, must be embedded in the organization's strategy at all levels.

Why Strategy Matters in Digital Transformation

Retailers offer a clear example. Consumers increasingly expect convenience—seamless purchasing from home or in-store, with the same level of service. A retailer that defines its strategy as "offering customers a 360-degree shopping experience across all channels" can then design its digital transformation around that promise. Product, operations, technology and external positioning, all aligned to support the strategy.

Without this clarity, transformation efforts scatter. Companies may invest millions in e-commerce platforms, apps, or marketing campaigns, but without a strategic anchor, those investments often lead to little more than digital noise, due to the disconnection between parties, especially amplified by siloed organizations that communicate very little.

Five Essential Questions of Strategy

Any solid business strategy should answer five fundamental questions:

1. Who are we going to serve?
   Which customers are we targeting? This includes both external customers who buy our products and internal customers (employees, departments) who enable the business to function and reach its objectives
2. What are we going to serve them?
   Which products or services do we want to offer? And crucially, which problems are we solving for them? Passion for our own products isn't enough, value must be defined through the customer's lens, knowing that it is a lot easier said than done, especially in larger companies, heavily consumer driven. Those products will differ based on consumer signals—but that, on its own, is a strategic choice too.
3. Why will they choose us?
   Why us, and not a competitor? What is our right to win? This is where competitive advantage is defined, and where investment focus becomes clear, aligning the whole narrative in a consistent way.

4. How are we going to serve them?

Through which channels, processes, and distribution models will we deliver on our promises? How do we guarantee consistency across touchpoints?

5. How will we ensure efficiency, effectiveness, and success?

What operational processes, organizational structures, and talent management practices will ensure we deliver sustainably and profitably

When leaders can answer these five questions, they hold the blueprint for a strategy that aligns all elements of digital transformation in the context of their overarching approach.

Common Pitfalls in Strategy

Many companies fail not because they lack resources but because they mistake activity for strategy. Some common pitfalls include:

- Mistaking projects for strategy: Implementing an ERP or launching an e-commerce site without linking it to broader business goals is a project not a strategic initiative.
- Copy-paste strategies: Simply replicating what competitors do, without considering unique context or differentiation
- Confusing efficiency with transformation: Cost cutting is not the same as creating future value.
- Short-term blindness: Chasing quarterly results while neglecting long-term positioning, often leading to missed market shifts

Blockbuster is the classic case study here. Their strategy revolved around maximizing revenue from late fees—a short-term objective. Netflix, in contrast, built a strategy around customer convenience and emerging technology. The rest is there to learn from.

Linking Strategy to the FRAME Pillars

Your strategy should also be tested against the FRAME pillars (Business Model, Market, Organization, Processes).

- *Who to serve?* → Market (Customers)
- *What to serve them?* → Business Model (Customers, Value Proposition)

- *Why us?* → Business Model (competitive advantage)
- *How to serve them?* → Organization (Technology, Operations, etc.) + Processes
- *How to ensure efficiency?* → Organization + Processes

By mapping strategy questions to the FRAME sequence, companies ensure that strategy is not an abstract statement but a practical foundation for transformation, connecting external perspective with the internal perspective.

Real-World Examples

Here are some real-world examples.

1. Amazon: Its strategy was not so much about "selling books." It was about being the most customer-centric company. That vision allowed it to expand across categories, from e-commerce to cloud computing, logistics, and beyond.
2. Airbnb: Its strategy was not necessarily "rent out rooms." It was creating authentic travel experiences, connecting travelers with unique stays. That guiding principle positioned Airbnb not as a hotel competitor but as a lifestyle enabler.
3. Bynco (Netherlands): Selling cars online wasn't about cars; it was about solving the problem of inconvenience in traditional car buying.

These examples show that strong strategies (and vision) transcend specific products, as they focus on problems to solve and value to deliver.

Practical Guidance for Leaders

For leaders designing a digital transformation strategy:

1. Test with the elevator pitch: Can you explain your strategy in 30 seconds, in a way that makes sense to employees and customers alike? If not, it's too complex or unfocused.

2. Check for alignment: Ensure that, like every substrategy (HR, operations, technology) flows directly from the company strategy.

3. Balance vision with adaptability: Strategy is not a five-year fixed plan; it's a living framework that adapts as markets shift.

4. Engage employees as internal customers: Strategy fails if the people who must execute it don't understand or believe in it.

How Do You Define Strategy's Success Measure?

One of the questions I am asked most often is: "How do we know if our strategy is working?"

My answer is always the same … by measuring it one way or another

A strategy without measurement is little more than wishful thinking. It is fine to declare that we want to "deliver better quality" or "serve customers better," but unless those aspirations are translated into tangible, trackable indicators (and connected), they cannot guide decision making.

Any company, regardless of its size, that embarks on digital transformation must define not only *what* wants to achieve but also *when* and *how progress will be tracked*. Strategy must be linked to measurable outcomes over defined time horizons—6 months, 12 months, 18 months, 24 months.

Practical Case: Shifting to a Subscription Model

Imagine a company that sells computer components through physical shops but wants to rethink its service to offer subscriptions for renting components, rather than only selling them. This is a strategic shift in the business model.

To succeed, the company must go beyond the vision ("we want to become the leading subscription service for computer components") and establish specific indicators to evaluate whether the strategy is producing results. For instance:

- Revenue Growth: Increase revenue volume by 15 percent within 18 months.
- Profitability: Improve operating margin by 27 percent within 24 months.

- Customer Experience: Raise Net Promoter Score (NPS) from 5 to 25 in the same period.
- Operational Efficiency: Reduce component repair rates by 40 percent.

These four indicators, while simple, provide a framework of success. They connect directly to the strategic intent and allow the company to evaluate progress objectively.

The Danger of "Fixed" Goals

However, one common mistake is treating these indicators as static, distant milestones. For example, aiming for 15 percent revenue growth in 18 months without intermediate checkpoints is risky. If performance drifts off track, the company might only realize too late.

Instead, strategy success requires continuous evaluation and agility. Incremental targets allow leaders to check "the pulse" of progress. In practice, this means setting smaller, measurable objectives that build toward the larger goal.

It could look like:

- Revenue should increase by 1 percent in the first two months,
- 2 percent by the fourth month,
- 5 percent by the eighth month,
- and so on, until the final 15 percent is achieved.

This incremental approach creates momentum, enables course correction, and ensures that the organization doesn't lose sight of the final destination.

Strategy as Doing, Not Saying

Roger Martin,[18] one of today's most respected strategy thinkers, puts it succinctly in his *Harvard Business Review* article: "Strategy isn't what you say, it's what you do."

---

[18]Roger L. Martin, "Strategy Isn't What You Say, It's What You Do," *Harvard Business Review*, June 18, 2014, https://hbr.org/2014/06/strategy-isnt-what-you-say-its-what-you-do.

This insight highlights the fundamental difference between vision and strategy. Vision is the story we tell—the "why" and the "north star." Strategy is the execution of that vision—the "how" and the "what we actually do."

Success, therefore, is not measured by the beautiful words of a vision statement, but by the tangible outcomes achieved when that vision is put in practice.

Digital transformation is not simply a technological renewal, but a paradigm shift. It redefines business models, customer relationships, operational processes, and employee experiences. This is why knowing how to measure strategic success is not optional, but the foundation for the sustainable transformation.

Final Thoughts

To conclude:

- Vision sets the direction.
- Strategy defines the path.
- Measurement ensures we are walking that path effectively.

A digital transformation without measurable outcomes risks becoming an endless project with no accountability. By defining strategy success with clear, incremental metrics, companies create the discipline to adjust, learn, and grow, ensuring their transformation efforts do not just start strong but also deliver lasting impact.

Business strategy is the connective link between vision and execution. In digital transformation, it is not optional, it is the guiding lens through which all investments, technologies, and operational changes must be seen. When companies confuse objectives with strategy, or treat IT as separate from strategy, they set themselves up for failure. When they design strategy around customer, problem, and value, aligning it with FRAME, they build a foundation for transformation that is both resilient and scalable.

CHAPTER 6

The Four-Floor Model

Transformation doesn't fail for lack of ideas or solutions, but, many times, for lack of a path. The Four-Floor Model is the ideal approach to help in building that path.

Over the last few chapters, we have explored different perspectives on what shapes a company undergoing transformation. One of the greatest challenges leaders face is how to bring it all together, aligning priorities, filtering what matters most, and defining a plan of action. It is not easy, but with structure, it becomes possible.

That is where the Four-Floor Model comes in and can help guiding you.

I developed this model to provide exactly that structure: *A way to take a vision and translate it into a clear set of initiatives that make the vision deliverable. It is a practical tool to guide decision making in digital transformation.* It applies equally well to any strategic or operational change.

Throughout my career, I have searched for models that not only helped me think about digital strategy in an integrated way but also helped my teams think the same way. The Four-Floor Model (illustrated in Figure 6.1) was born out of this need.

At its core, the model breaks down the process of creating an implementation plan into 4 + 1 phases: four structured "floors" plus a planning phase (covered in a later chapter). Each floor builds logically on the previous one, always starting with the vision of the company, product, or service we aim to create or improve.

A Vision in Action: Maersk

In 2016, Soren Skou, CEO of A.P. Moller-Maersk, announced a bold new strategy: Maersk would stop being a conglomerate and transform into an integrated logistics company—offering end-to-end logistics

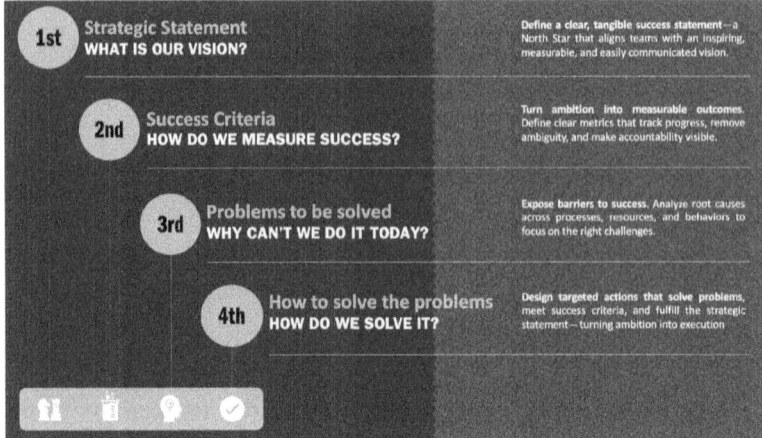

Figure 6.1 The Four-Floor Model infographic

from the factory in remote countries to the consumer's doorstep. When he introduced this strategy, Skou expressed his vision in a striking way: "Maersk will make the process of buying logistics services as simple as buying a plane ticket."

At first, this statement may have sounded like a slogan. But soon after, it became a filter for every decision inside the company. From that point forward, each initiative was tested against a single question: *Does this make the process as simple as buying a plane ticket?*

This is exactly what the Four-Floor Model is designed to achieve: turning vision into action through structured decision making.

Broad and Granular Applications

The model works at both macro and micro levels. It can start with a companywide vision, as in Maersk's case, but it is just as effective for more specific purposes, such as:

- Launching a new product
- Launching a new company
- Driving an operational restructuring project

In both cases, the need is the same: Define the activities that will turn the vision through clear success measures.

Two Key Applications

Later in this book, we will also explore how the Four-Floor Model can be applied in two powerful contexts:

- Strategy Design—Using the model to structure what is needed to realize an end-to-end strategy
- Investment Analysis—Using the model's outcomes to evaluate the investments required to implement the strategy

The Four Floors

The model structures this process step by step:

1. The First Floor—Define a vision for the company, product, or project.
2. The Second Floor—Define the measurable results that will determine success.
3. The Third Floor—Identify the problem preventing these results today.
4. The Fourth Floor—Define the initiatives, activities, or projects that will solve the problems.

The outcome is a clear map that connects vision → measurable results → obstacles → concrete initiatives.

Ambition needs architecture. The Four-Floor Model turns vision into execution by defining success, surfacing problems, and sequencing initiatives into a path we can follow.

The First Floor

Every journey starts with a destination. For a company, a business unit, or even a single product, that destination is the vision. The First Floor of the model forces us to pause and ask: *Where are we heading, and what will success look like in the eyes of our customers?*

This step is about creating a collective vision—one that everyone can understand and rally behind. It should be simple enough to repeat without a presentation yet bold enough to inspire action. The goal is clarity: a statement that tells teams, investors, and customers alike what the end product or service will *deliver*.

Think of some of the most memorable examples of corporate vision:

1. Microsoft (early 1980s): "A computer on every desk and in every home."
2. Google: "To organize the world's information and make it universally accessible and useful."
3. Tesla: "To accelerate the world's transition to sustainable energy."
4. IKEA: "To create a better everyday life for the many people."

Each of these visions is short, easy to remember, and powerful enough to guide thousands of daily decisions. They don't explain *how* the company will achieve the vision—that comes later. Instead, they set the guideline that shapes priorities and filters choices.

Too often, companies—especially start-ups—fail because they fall in love with what *they* want to build rather than what customers truly need. The discipline of the First Floor exists to prevent exactly that mistake. It compels organizations to anchor strategy in customer reality, not founder preference.

And yet, this is often the hardest floor to implement. Many companies are rich in operational talent but poor in vision-setting talent. The urgent pulls of daily operations can drown out the deeper question of direction. Without vision, however, activity becomes motion without progress.

I have seen this firsthand. In large organizations, strategy teams can spend months perfecting financial models and execution plans while never daring to answer the simple but uncomfortable question: *What are we trying to become?* In smaller firms, founders sometimes define vision only for investors—turning it into a pitch rather than a genuine compass. In both cases, teams end up working hard but without shared clarity.

The First Floor does not require pages of strategy documents. What it requires is focus—a crisp statement of intent that can act as a guiding line for all that follows. From this line, the next step becomes possible: asking, *How will we measure success against this vision?*

That is the role of the Second Floor.

The Second Floor

If the First Floor is about defining *where we want to go*, the Second Floor is about defining *how we know when we've arrived.*

This is the step of turning a vision into success criteria—objectives and results that are tangible enough to measure, realistic enough to achieve, and ambitious enough to stretch the organization beyond the immediate horizon.

The Nature of Objectives

Not all objectives are created equal. Some are financial, some are operational, and some are customer-experience driven. The important thing is that they are:

- Tangible—clear enough to measure
- Meaningful—connected to the vision
- Time-balanced—not only short-term but tied to a medium-to-long-term trajectory

Digital transformations, in particular, are medium-term by nature. They rarely deliver full success in a single quarter, so objectives should avoid being too immediate. That said, certain short-term objectives can matter when they have intrinsic value for the longer journey.

For example, EBITDA (earnings before interest, taxes, depreciation, and amortization) is often seen as a financial objective tied to short-term decisions such as cost cutting. But in the context of transformation, it can also serve as a proxy for operational efficiency—an indicator of how much value the company can generate per unit of sales. This kind of efficiency can, in turn, unlock reinvestment in innovation or improved customer service.

There is no universal formula for choosing the "right" objectives. A useful rule of thumb is to select those that balance two perspectives:

1. The customer's perspective—Does this objective make the product or service more valuable, faster, or easier to use?
2. The company's health—Does it strengthen financial resilience, operational efficiency, or long-term competitiveness?

A strong set of objectives incorporates both.

Let's go back to Soren Skou's vision for Maersk, which was to "make buying logistics services as simple as buying a plane ticket."

Maersk could use conventional financial indicators like operating margins or revenue growth to define success at the corporate level. However, more precise outcomes are necessary when converting the vision into product-level requirements.

Consider a Maersk logistics booking team. They could set a goal like, "Provide container ship pricing and availability in less than two seconds," in order to fulfill the "as simple as a plane ticket" vision.

Revenue may not be directly generated by this goal alone. But it makes the customer experience much better by making the process quick, clear, and trustworthy.

From Success to Problems

Defining objectives also begins to surface the gaps and problems that stand in the way of achieving them. If "two-second availability" is the target, then delays in data processing, fragmented IT systems, or lack of automation quickly emerge as problems.

And this is where the model naturally moves to the Third Floor: identifying the problems that prevent us from delivering the results we've defined.

The Third Floor

If the Second Floor establishes the goals that signify achievement, the Third Floor compels us to face the challenges that stand in our way. In short, it provides an answer to the query, "What keeps us from accomplishing these goals today?"

Here, aspiration and reality collide.

From Goals to Shortfalls

Consider a logistics company whose goal is to deliver 95 percent of cargo on time. The "problem" doesn't exist if the business is already meeting or surpassing its goal at 95 percent. However, there is a 20 percent discrepancy between the current performance and the specified goal if it is only delivering 75 percent on time.

However, that number isn't the issue itself. It's just the symptom. There could be a number of underlying problems behind it:

1. Insufficient operational resources
2. Insufficient real-time information exchange
3. Disjointed departmental procedures

This step is valuable because it converts deficiencies into concrete, diagnosable problems. As long as we keep asking, "Why can't we deliver this result now?" it is likely we will keep identifying various problems that are critical to achieve the results.

Why Knowing the Problems Matter

Based on my experience, this exercise frequently reveals an unsettling reality: Certain visions are just not possible given the limitations.

Although it's common knowledge that "everything has a solution," not all of them are useful or feasible in real life. It is much better to realize early on that a vision is unachievable than to spend years of effort in the wrong direction. If the common saying "better late than never" is accurate, I also like to say *better sooner than later*.

Breaking Down Problems

Some issues are too big to be resolved directly. When that occurs, a large problem can be reduced to a mini Four-Floor process by using the model itself recursively.

Take the issue, "We can't serve large customers with our current sales force" as an example. This is too complicated to handle in a single step. Alternatively, it could be rephrased as a subvision like this: "We want a sales force that is close to customers, dynamic, and acts as a partner rather than just a vendor."

New goals (like relationship depth or customer satisfaction ratings) can then be established, and the particular issues impeding these results (like inadequate relationship management training) can be addressed. This makes it possible to divide the big, abstract problem into more manageable, smaller ones.

Clearly Defining Problems

Clarity is this floor's primary success factor. An effective problem statement is:

1. Tangible: We know when is resolved.
2. Specific: It stays away from ambiguous phrases like "too slow" and "not efficient enough."
3. Contextual: It has a clear connection to the goals and vision.

See this example

- Vague: "Our operations aren't quick enough."
- Clearly stated: "Our goal is two hours; order processing takes twelve hours."

Staying Out of the Solution Trap

There is a strong temptation to jump straight to solutions at this point. However, the Third Floor isn't meant for solution mode. Prior to defining the initiatives that will address the issues on the Fourth Floor, the discipline is to remain focused on identifying the actual problems.

Crucially, a large number of these problems will be more than just technical in nature. They frequently have to do with processes, organizations, or culture. Although technology might eventually play a role in the solution, the Third Floor focuses on diagnosis rather than prescription.

From Problems to Initiatives

The second the foundation is laid with a concise list of verified problems, we can then start asking what is needed to address those.

That's what the Fourth Floor is all about.

The Fourth Floor

The model transitions from diagnosis to action on the Fourth Floor. The Fourth Floor poses the following query if the Third Floor identifies the problems that hinder success:

"What actions, projects or initiatives can we do to address those problems?"

The answer will eventually feed the roadmap's fundamental units.

From Problems to Initiatives

Consider a retailer that is looking to expand its business model to allow consumers to collect orders in the store, and one of the problems they have is that "it is not possible for the store associates to know what orders are to be prepared and collected." One of the ways to solve this problem (oversimplified) is straightforward: Install the required software in priority stores to enable in-store collection if the issue is that customers are unable to pick up online orders in-store because some stores do not have the necessary software.

Or consider the situation where a clothing company does not have integrations with local logistics providers, so it is unable to accept returns from overseas. Creating a digital product that links the brand's platform with regional logistics providers to facilitate cross-border returns could be the corresponding initiative.

The initiative stems directly from the issue in both situations. At this point, selecting a particular vendor or technology is not important; that is for later. Here, the emphasis is on outlining the overarching initiatives that tackle the identified problems, that when implemented, will eliminate the challenges noted on the Third Floor. Of course, it doesn't need to be always in this level of magnitude (new large systems). It can also be a retailer that already provides click and collect but has an issue with store associates rejecting the orders due to fear of not having stock for normal walk-in orders. To solve this problem, it is much more about providing them the right level of information to make an informed decision, rather than fear, which may connect to a success measure of "# of orders rejected," that is intended to be reduced, that connects to a product vision of "The channel that never turns down an order"

Connecting Initiatives to the Vision

The Four-Floor Model's traceability is one of its advantages. If you are disciplined, you can trace each Fourth Floor initiative back to:

- A problem (the Third Floor),
- A success criterion (the Second Floor),
- And ultimately, the vision (the First Floor).

One-to-one mapping is not required. A single issue may very well break down to multiple initiatives, or a single initiative may tackle multiple problems

The important thing is that initiatives always have a direct path back to the vision.

Comparing Financial and Functional Viability

It is crucial to stress that the Four-Floor Model is not intended to determine financial viability or return on investment. Instead, by outlining the necessary steps, it aims to make the vision operationally feasible. Initiatives can be evaluated for cost, return, and prioritization during the planning stage after they have been identified.

Stated differently:

- "What needs to be done?" is the response from the Fourth Floor.
- The question, "Is it worth doing?" is addressed by financial analysis.

When Initiatives Turn into Visions

Occasionally, a Fourth Floor initiative is too big and strategic to be handled as a single action. In these situations, it serves as the beginning of a fresh Four-Floor cycle.

An initiative is a vision unto itself, for instance, if it is described as "launching a new digital product line." It can be reorganized into goals, issues, and projects on the First Floor of a new submodel.

A hierarchy of submodels is produced by this recursive application of the model:

- The overarching goal
- Divided into significant initiatives
- Each of which can be further broken down into more manageable plans and initiatives, by converting into a vision statement that ultimately turns into a broken down connected Four Floors

When using the Four-Floor Model at the corporate level, where big projects need to be broken down into more specific plans, this method is especially helpful.

The Fourth Floor's Output

At the conclusion of this floor, the organization will have:

- A list of initiatives that specifically address the problems identified
- An unambiguous link to the vision
- A series of submodels for major initiatives, if needed

The planning phase, which analyzes financial viability, prioritization, and sequencing, is built upon these initiatives taken together.

In summary, the Fourth Floor solves the problems identified in the Third Floor by creating a workable plan that realizes the goal of the First Floor, measured through the Second Floor.

Practice Case: The Four-Floor Model

To illustrate how the Four-Floor Model works in practice, let's walk through a simple, oversimplified, high-level scenario. The example is not meant to capture the full complexity of digital transformation. Instead, this case shows how the model can be applied step by step, moving from vision to initiatives in a structured way.

Our fictional company, Step Right Shoes, is a midsize shoe retailer with 500 employees. Until now, Step Right has focused exclusively on physical stores. But with shifting customer behavior, rising competition, and declining in-store sales, the company realizes it must move into digital channels. Using the Four-Floor Model, we can demonstrate how Step Right defines its vision, translates it into measurable objectives, identifies the key problems, and finally, builds a roadmap of initiatives that make the digital shift possible.

The First Floor—Vision

The company needs a bold but clear direction to unite employees around digital transformation. After several workshops with leadership, employees, and customer insights, they define the vision: "Step Right Shoes will make buying shoes online as personal and effortless as visiting our stores."

This vision is customer-focused, easy to understand, and acts as a guiding line: Everything the company does digitally must bring the convenience of online shopping together with the personal touch of in-store service.

The Second Floor—Success Criteria

The next step is to translate this vision into measurable results. For Step Right, success might mean:

1. Customer Experience
   1. Customers can browse, select, and purchase shoes online in under five minutes.
   2. Online customers rate their experience 4.5 or higher.
2. Sales and Reach
   - Twenty-five percent of total revenue to come from digital channels within three years
   - Online platform to serve customers in 10 countries within three years
3. Operational Efficiency
   - Ninety-eight percent of online orders fulfilled on time
   - Returns processed within three days

These objectives strike a balance between customer value and company health.

The Third Floor—Problems

Now, Step Right identifies the obstacles preventing those objectives today. For example:

1. Customer Experience Gap
   - We have no integrated online store, other than a simple online catalog on our website.
   - Product catalog not digitized (inventory only available in-store systems).
   - We lack clear data from our consumers to make it personal.
2. Sales and Reach Gap
   - Lack of digital marketing expertise in-house
3. Operational Efficiency Gap
   - Our logistics processes are not catered for parcel processing.
   - We have no visibility toward online orders coming to warehouse.
   - Logistic providers and stores not integrated for "click and collect."

Each of these problems creates the deficit between the current state and the defined objectives.

The Fourth Floor—Initiatives

Finally, initiatives are defined to solve these problems. For Step Right, the roadmap includes:

1. Customer Experience Initiatives
   - Launch a modern but simple e-commerce platform integrated with inventory.
   - Digitize the full product catalog with high-quality images, sizing guides, and fit recommendations.

○ Implement personalization features (AI-based product suggestions, virtual try-on).

2. Sales and Reach Initiatives
   ○ Build a digital marketing team or outsource (SEO [search engine optimization], social media, performance marketing).
   ○ Expand e-commerce to three countries in year 1, scaling to 10 by year 3.

3. Operational Initiatives
   ○ Integrate logistic providers and store systems for unified inventory management.
   ○ Build "click and collect" functionality for all stores.
   ○ Develop a returns portal connected to logistics partners to handle cross-border returns.

Some initiatives are large enough to become submodels themselves. For example, "launch a modern e-commerce platform" is not just a project, it is a new vision in itself. It can be reframed into a Four-Floor submodel (Vision: seamless digital store; Objectives: uptime, performance, customer adoption; Problems: integration gaps, UX weaknesses; Initiatives: platform selection, design, testing).

If you thought, "Of course it looks very simple, but in real-life is more complex," you are correct. The example I gave is far oversimplified. It is only an attempt demonstrate the idea. The reality, can be more broken down, can be more targeted, can be more specific. However, the purpose of this chapter is to foster the thinking behind, rather than show an exact example. That's also an important take away. The highest level you start (company, product, feature, etc.), the hardest it will be to make it that granular, and likely will create more submodels.

Limitations and Ideal Cases

Just like any other model, it also has its own limitations (some examples):

- Better fit for smaller units than for larger units. As explained, if the vision is about building an entire new company merging two large companies, this type of model can be quite complex to apply. It can be used to foster the dialogue, but it is unlikely you can frame it all in a single Four-Floor Model.

- In very large companies, it could become quite overwhelming to manage from top strategy down to five or six levels down in this structure, hence not very suitable.

It is, however, a great fit for other situations (some examples):

- Build a new a disruptive feature of an existing product, where we can clearly define a vision, measures, problems and initiatives in a very contained approach.
- Launch a new product, allowing to be very clear on what is needed to make that product vision a success.
- Deconstruct a transformation in multiple vision statements, and each statement being defined by this model, as this allows to slide the large transformation in smaller pieces.

The Four-Floor Model and Strategy?

The Four-Floor Model is not a strategy in itself. Rather, it is a tool that supports the strategy process by providing structure, clarity, and traceability.

Strategy is often described as "eating the elephant one bite at a time." That is exactly what the Four-Floor Model enables: starting with the vision and progressively breaking it down into measurable objectives, concrete problems, and actionable initiatives.

When applied at the strategic level, the model works like a cascade:

- Vision—the company's overarching ambition
- Objectives—the outcomes that define success
- Problems—the barriers preventing those outcomes
- Initiatives—the roadmap of actions that solve the problems

From there, submodels can be created. A problem that is too large, or an initiative that is too complex, can become the starting point for a new Four-Floor cycle. In this way, strategy is deconstructed into smaller, tangible maps, each still fully connected to the original vision.

The great strength of this approach is integration. Whether you are working four or five levels down—in a product team, a functional area, or a regional unit—every initiative can still be traced back to the company's vision. This ensures alignment, avoids wasted effort, and prevents local projects from drifting away from strategic priorities.

For many organizations, the challenge is not ambition but structure. Too often, objectives are mistaken for strategy, or activities are pursued without clarity on how they contribute to the whole. The Four-Floor Model creates a map of strategy in action:

- A hierarchy that translates ambition into initiatives
- A way to delegate ownership of submodels to different leadership levels
- A foundation for linking functional viability to financial viability

Ultimately, the Four-Floor Model does not replace the work of defining strategy. What it does is make strategy tangible and executable. It shows not only where you want to go but also how you will get there—and ensures that every action taken along the way remains aligned with the vision at the top.

Analyzing Investments

The Four-Floor Model is more than just a tool for organizing goals, challenges, and projects. By connecting each initiative to the vision and its potential value, it also serves as a basis for investment analysis.

When looking at investments, I suggest that you think of the company's change as a whole cake instead of separate slices.

That number becomes the starting point for making decisions if the vision is expected to bring in, say, €200 million more in value. It shows the highest level of possible gains. Starting from this point, we can figure out the most money that can be put into a business case that will still work.

For example:

1. If the vision is worth €200 million,
2. The total cost of projects on all Four Floors must stay below €200 million, ideally well below that, say hypothetically €150 million.

The number would depend on how many other factors like net present value expected, cash flow, and so on. This is only to represent the idea that if one is clear what is the measurable return of a specific vision (Four-Floor Model), then the total investment to be distributed by initiatives, can be better defined.

The list of initiatives is on the Fourth Floor. The total of their costs tells you how much money you need to invest. Adding up their expected gains gives them the value pool they can access. The business case falls apart if the total costs are higher than the baseline value.

At that point, leaders can choose between two things:

- Make the portfolio more efficient by getting rid of or changing projects that cost a lot but don't add much value.
- Look at the vision again. If there is no way to make it happen, you may need to change the vision itself or drop it.

Both are good results. It is better to decide early that a change is not possible than to lose a lot more later.

Common Mistakes in Investment Analysis

When using this method, three common mistakes happen:

- Weak Visions: If the first vision is not clear or well-defined, the investment logic falls apart. It's hard for small businesses to come up with a vision that is both specific and aspirational enough to help with financial analysis.
- Short-Termism: A lot of companies put more weight on urgent short-term problems than on goals that will take longer to reach. You can't just look at quarterly gains to justify digital

transformations. Companies that don't balance their horizons risk making choices that hurt their long-term viability.

- Lack of Support: Even the best investment case can fail if the organization doesn't agree with it. Leaders need to talk about more than just the numbers; they need to talk about the story behind the numbers—why this vision is important, how it affects customers, and what it means for every part of the business.

Going Back to the Point of Success

You can't separate investment analysis from customer value. A vision must always address a genuine issue. If Maersk hadn't realized that booking logistics services was a frustrating and complicated process for its customers, its vision of "as simple as a plane ticket" would have gone nowhere, no matter how good the business case looked on paper.

A Process That Lives

Finally, you don't just do investment analysis once. Technologies advance, markets shift, and consumer expectations increase. You will have to go back and look at the assumptions you made at the start of a change. The problem isn't making mistakes but rather not learning from them and failing to adapt.

The Four-Floor Model keeps the investment case connected to the real world by making sure that as visions change, goals are set, and initiatives are changed, they are still based on what customers need, what the company can deliver, and what is financially possible.

CHAPTER 7

The Disruption Through Technology

Technology is no longer a support function; it is the logic of competition. Disruption rarely arrives as a shock—it advances quietly as new services, new expectations, and new ways to create value. We begin with the Digital Services Economy, where firms orchestrate platforms and partners instead of owning every link in the chain. We then unpack how disruption climbs "from below," and why a digital twin can let incumbents reinvent themselves at start-up speed. From there, we look at globalization and digital commerce—the great equalizers that expand reach but raise the bar on brand, logistics, and focus. Finally, we examine generative AI as a cocreator that amplifies differentiation when used with purpose. This chapter closes with practical guidance: principles for making technology decisions that endure, and a hypothesis-driven strategy to test assumptions before scaling. The message is simple: Every company is now a technology company. The advantage goes to those who are clear about where they create value—and disciplined about everything else.

The Digital Services Economy

It's second nature to sign up for services these days. We pay for things like entertainment, moving, food delivery, cloud storage, and even furniture. People used to think that some services were "special," but now they can get them whenever they want, often in real time. Not only has technology changed, but the way we think about making money has changed too.

This change is the basis for what I call the Digital Services Economy. In this economy, businesses don't need to own, build, or even run many parts of their value chain directly. They don't provide services themselves;

instead, they coordinate services that others do. These services are digital, scalable, and flexible.

From Software Licenses to Everything as a Service

Software-as-a-Service (SaaS) was the fundamental step in this change. For years, businesses bought software on CDs, paid for licenses, installed it on servers, and went through long, painful upgrade cycles. A lot of people will remember typing in activation codes for Windows or Office over and over again.

This changed when cloud computing came along. Salesforce.com, which started in 1999, was one of the first companies to offer enterprise-level software only as a web service. Companies no longer had to keep servers up to date or install updates all of a sudden. They signed up. They were more interested in using the software than keeping it up to date.

This way of thinking spread quickly. We now talk about XaaS, which stands for "Everything as a Service." With Infrastructure-as-a-Service (IaaS), you can rent computing power. Platform-as-a-Service (PaaS) gives you ready-made spaces to build and grow apps. There are real things like Logistics-as-a-Service (LaaS), Payments-as-a-Service, and even HR-as-a-Service. A specialist platform can now handle almost any part of a business's work.

What does this mean? The value chain has been broken up. Companies don't have to do everything themselves anymore; they can choose where to focus and where to connect to existing platforms.

Two Types of Services in the Digital Economy

1. Platform as a Provider
   The company gives the service directly to the customer. For example, Netflix (for streaming content) or Amazon Web Services (for infrastructure). They own the service and how it works.
2. Platform as a marketplace
   The business links customers with service providers. Airbnb and Uber don't own hotels or cars. These businesses manage supply and demand on a large scale.

Both models shake up existing businesses by getting rid of bottle-necks, making it easier for new businesses to get in, and making it easier to get to services.

Strategic Effects on Businesses

The services economy has deep effects in businesses. Here are five key insights to consider in my view:

1. Concentrate on core specialization
   Businesses need to figure out what they are really good at and then get rid of the rest. Restaurants shouldn't waste time and money try-ing to build delivery fleets. Instead, they should focus on the qual-ity of their food, how it is packaged, and how customers feel about their experience. Logistics companies might hire someone else to do the last mile delivery, but they should focus on supply chain analyt-ics. Now the question is not, "What can we do?" but, "What do we have to do to stay relevant?"

2. Be careful of commoditization
   Platforms make things fair. If every restaurant can be on Uber Eats, delivery is no longer a unique feature. If every store can open a Shopify store, e-commerce is no longer a good thing. Differen-tiation needs to move to areas where platforms can't make things cheap, like brand, experience, trust, and specialized knowledge.

3. Partner orchestration as a key skill
   Leaders must become orchestrators in a value chain that is broken up. It's less important to have every skill and more important to bring together different services into a single, smooth whole. The best companies create modular ecosystems by outsourcing tasks that don't set them apart but making sure that the whole experience feels like one.

4. Not resistance, but reinvention
   The travel industry is a warning. Booking.com and Skyscanner, for example, changed the game for agencies by giving customers more information and power. Many agencies fought back and stuck to their old way of doing things. Others changed their business

models to focus on specific markets, like high-end travel or personalized experiences. The difference is that accepting that disruption doesn't take away all value, but changes where value is.

5. Scaling without owning

This is especially good for start-ups. Shopify for commerce, Stripe for payments, AWS for hosting, and DHL for logistics all make it possible for a small brand to grow all over the world without having to own a single server or delivery truck. This makes it much easier to get in, but it also makes the competition much stronger. The question is: What extra benefit do you offer on top of the platform?

Examples from Different Fields:

- Retail: Independent sellers don't need physical stores as much as they needed before. They can reach customers all over the world through platforms like Etsy, Amazon, or Wish. But success doesn't come from "being present"; it comes from building a brand, telling stories, and finding a niche.
- Logistics: Fulfillment by Amazon (FBA) made shipping and warehousing a service. Small businesses can go global in a day. Traditional logistics companies that depend on long contracts need to rethink how they do business.
- Hospitality: Airbnb changed the market from "hotels" to "places to stay." The competition grew; now a spare bedroom could compete with a five-star hotel. Incumbents had to rethink what loyalty, service, and unique experiences meant.
- Automotive: Sites like Bynco let people buy cars online. The problem with the car wasn't the value; it was the buying process. Whoever fixes the process issue gets the customer.

The Next Wave: Services AI Is What Makes It Work

The economy of services is moving into a new phase. Generative AI makes it possible for services to learn, change, and personalize in real time. Instead of static marketplaces, we will see platforms that automatically improve processes, guess what customers want, and cut down on the need for people to get involved.

Picture customer service as a service that is run entirely by AI agents that learn your company's tone and rules. Or AI-driven financial services that automatically set budgets, find the best tax rates, and predict risks. These aren't far-off futures; they're being tested right now.

Why This Is Important for Digital Change

The Digital Services Economy is not about outsourcing everything. It is about focusing where you create true value, and leverage platforms where you do not.

For larger companies, the challenge is cultural, by letting go of control and reinventing legacy processes. For small companies, the challenge is strategic, by avoiding becoming invisible in a sea of similar offerings.

The rule of thumb is simple:

- Do fewer things but do them better.
- Outsource the rest to digital services.
- Orchestrate the ecosystem so customers experience one coherent brand, not a patchwork of providers.

Digital transformation in this era is about mastering the art of orchestration. The companies that succeed will be those who embrace platforms not as threats but as enablers of focus, scale, and speed.

Silent Disruption and Digital Twins

Disruption is one of the most overused words in business today, yet it remains one of the least understood. Many executives nod when the term is mentioned, but few grasp the quiet, almost invisible way in which it often unfolds. By the time disruption is obvious, it is usually too late.

To truly understand disruption, we must go back to work of Clayton Christensen,[19] the Harvard professor who reshaped the way we think

---

[19] Clayton M. Christensen, *The Innovator's Dilemma: When New Technologies Cause Great Firms to Fail* (Harvard Business School Press, 1997).

about products, markets, and customers. Christensen's Jobs to Be Done theory placed the customer's problem, rather than the company's product, at the center of strategy. But his greatest contribution may be how he explained the *mechanics* of disruption: It rarely comes head-on. Instead, it sneaks in "from below."

The Ladder of Sophistication

Christensen showed that new entrants typically begin by serving less demanding customers—those whose needs are simple, whose expectations are low, or whose willingness to pay is limited. Established players dismiss these customers as unprofitable, not worth their time. The new entrants start here because it is easier, cheaper, and less competitive.

Over time, however, these entrants climb the ladder of sophistication. They improve their offerings, add more features, and begin to attract customers higher up the market. By then, incumbents often discover that they are losing share not at the fringes, but at the very core of their business.

What makes digital disruption particularly dangerous is that companies starting at the bottom often begin with a technological advantage. They build on scalable cloud architectures, gather data from the start, and move quickly in cycles of testing and iteration. By the time they reach the higher rungs of the ladder, their foundation is stronger than that of the incumbents.

One of the most dangerous behaviors in incumbents is arrogance toward smaller challengers. A century-old firm looks at a start-up of 20 people and thinks, *they can't possibly threaten us*. But markets are not static. What starts as a small player with a niche offer can grow into a category leader if it solves problems more effectively.

By the time large firms recognize the threat, the gap may be impossible to close. Their technology is fragmented, their culture resistant, and their processes optimized for yesterday's model. Meanwhile, the disruptor has already captured the imagination of the market.

Another subtle aspect of disruption is that new entrants often create demand that didn't exist before. Take food delivery platforms. Restaurants had always offered delivery, but it was clunky: Each operated its own system, and customers had to choose between dozens of different websites or phone calls. Then came Uber Eats, Deliveroo, and Take Away. Suddenly, consumers could access hundreds of restaurants in one place.

No one had been marching in the streets asking for this solution. But once it existed, consumers demanded more: faster delivery, better packaging, more choice. Disruption doesn't just respond to demand; it reshapes expectations and redefines what "good" looks like.

Incumbents fail not because they cannot see disruption coming but because they cannot act at the right speed. They are tied to legacy operations, long-term contracts, and entrenched ways of working. The very success that made them strong becomes their weakness.

Unlike digital-native entrants, they often lack:

- Scalable technology foundations (cloud, APIs, data pipelines)
- Agile feedback loops to learn quickly from customers
- Cultural readiness to question old models and cannibalize their own revenue streams

The result is a slow, painful recognition that change is needed—often when it is already too late.

But If disruption is silent and stealthy, how can companies prepare? I see three dimensions as essential:

- Embed digital into business strategy. Technology cannot be a support function. It must be part of the core strategy, as central as finance or operations. Without it, scaling against disruptors is impossible.
- Continuously monitor the market. Especially the start-up ecosystem. Silent disruption almost always begins at the fringes, with what incumbents consider irrelevant. Constant scanning helps detect weak signals before they become tidal waves.
- Experiment with digital twins. Perhaps the most powerful response: Create a parallel company, lighter and fully digital, to compete on new terms. When reinventing the core is too difficult, build something alongside it that can.

Disruption will never stop. It is not a one-off threat but a permanent feature of markets in the digital age. The only question is whether companies treat it as a risk to be defended against, or as an opportunity to be created.

That brings us to the concept of digital twins—a strategy that allows established companies to disrupt themselves before others do. How fascinating that is?

Digital Twin for Companies Already in the Market (or Digital Twin)

Digital twins are perhaps the most practical and radical way for established companies with resources to rethink how they compete. The term was popularized in engineering, but in a business context it refers to creating a parallel company—one that operates with the speed, agility, and customer focus of a start-up but benefits from the knowledge and assets of the parent company.

As Grieves and Vickers,[20] digital twins help mitigate the complexity that prevents established organizations from transforming themselves. Instead of trying to overhaul a legacy organization in one painful move, the company builds a new one alongside it.

At its simplest, a digital twin is like starting over. It is building a start-up inside or beside the company: same industry, same customer needs, but with a completely new model. Free from legacy processes, entrenched systems, and old habits, the twin can compete directly with disruptors on their terms.

It is not an innovation lab, a pilot team, or a side project. It is a full business with its own operations, culture, and P&L. Its purpose is to attack the lower end of the market before competitors do and then scale upward with a technological advantage.

Christensen himself warned how hard it is for incumbents to reinvent themselves. They have to keep serving their existing customers

---

[20]Michael Grieves and John Vickers, "Digital Twin: Mitigating Unpredictable, Undesirable Emergent Behavior in Complex Systems," in *Trans-Disciplinary Perspectives on System Complexity*, ed. F.-J. Kahlen, S. Flumerfelt, and A. Alves (Springer, 2017), 85–113.

while experimenting with new models. They are prisoners of their own success.

A digital twin solves this paradox:

- The parent company continues serving established, profitable customers.
- The twin company serves new, less profitable segments with a lean, digital model.

Over time, the twin climbs the ladder of sophistication, while the parent focuses on high-value segments. Together, they cover the market more effectively, or eventually, the twin may even assume its role as the main business. It all depends on how it evolves.

A Practical Example

Consider a consultancy of 300 employees with 3,000 clients in real estate. It acts as an intermediary, helping clients find properties via its relationships with agencies. The model is people-heavy and relationship-driven.

But this is exactly the kind of business ripe for disruption: Much of what it does can be digitalized, using data and algorithms to match clients with properties faster and more cheaply.

How could a digital twin work?

- Segment the customer base. Which clients require highly specialized, high-touch services? Which simply want quick, standardized help?
- Identify underserved groups. Are there potential clients outside the base who need low-cost, self-service options?
- Design the twin. Build a platform that automates matching, integrates listings, and allows clients to self-serve.

At first, the twin addresses only the low-end, low-margin clients. But over time, with continuous improvement, it becomes attractive even to higher segments.

Outcomes of the Digital Twin Approach

1. Margin focus. The parent company improves gross margins by focusing on premium segments, while the twin scales efficiently in the mid- to low-end.
2. Operational efficiency. Resources are used more effectively: Fewer people needed for basic services, more deployed to complex cases.
3. Risk management. The company essentially disrupts itself before others do, keeping both ends of the ladder covered.

Barriers to Digital Twins

Of course, digital twins are not without challenges:

1. Capital requirements. Building a parallel business requires investment that small firms may lack.
2. Cultural resistance. Leaders may fear cannibalization, or employees may resist a "new rival" inside the company.
3. Execution risk. Without clear separation, the twin risks being dragged back into the parent's old ways.

Yet these barriers are often less dangerous than the alternative: doing nothing and letting external disruptors eat away at the business.

Who Can Use This Approach?

While digital twins are often recommended for established companies, start-ups can adopt the mindset too. They can build multiple versions of themselves to attack different customer segments. In both cases, the principle is the same: Create a structure that solves problems in new ways before someone else does.

Final Thoughts

Digital twins are not just a defensive play—they are an offensive strategy. They allow incumbents to play the start-up game while retaining the credibility and resources of an established brand. In a world of silent disruption, they might be the best chance a company has to survive—and to thrive.

The Digital Shortcut to Globalization

We live in a global world. With access to technology, competition is no longer limited to the rival down the street; it is with companies across the continent—and often across the globe. What once required years of expansion, investment, and risk is now possible with just a few digital tools and platforms.

Globalization is not a new phenomenon, but its pace, scope, and accessibility have been radically accelerated by digitalization. The link between the two has been widely studied in recent years. In a 2019 article, Yan-Yin Lee et al.[21] highlighted the clear relationship between digitalization and internationalization, emphasizing that companies must invest in competences that enable international growth, and that digitalization is one of the most powerful accelerators of that process. Similarly, in 2020, Annaële Hervé et al.[22] concluded that there is a direct link between the degree of digitalization and the degree of internationalization in small and medium enterprises (SMEs), reinforcing that digital transformation is not just an efficiency play but a gateway to new markets.

I begin with these references because they highlight a truth that leaders must not ignore: digitalization, globalization, and internationalization go hand in hand. And yet, many companies still see these as separate domains, when in fact they are inseparable.

With technology evolving at speed, barriers that once defined markets have almost disappeared:

- It is now common for someone to work remotely from Madrid for a company in New York or Singapore.

---

[21]Yan-Yin Lee, Mohammad Falahat, and Bik-Kai Sia, "Impact of Digitalization on the Speed of Internationalization," *International Business Research* 12, no. 4 (2019): 1–11.
[22]Annaële Hervé, Christophe Schmitt, and Rico Baldegger, "Digitalization, Entrepreneurial Orientation and Internationalization of Micro-, Small-, and Medium-Sized Enterprises," *Technology Innovation Management Review* 10, no. 4 (2020): 5–17.

- Any company can provide services to global customers without leaving their local city.
- R&D centers are increasingly located in emerging economies like India, Indonesia, or the Philippines, leveraging talent pools that were once inaccessible.
- Consumers travel internationally at affordable prices, bringing with them expectations for global brands, seamless digital experiences, and consistent service.

The pandemic amplified this shift dramatically. In 2016, when I joined the Maersk Group, it was a challenge to hold a video call with more than six people. By 2020, thousands of employees were collaborating virtually, and consumers were ordering online in volumes that were equivalent to 10 years of e-commerce growth compressed into months. Technology pulled countries, companies, and customers closer together.

This reality is both an opportunity and a challenge. For vast majority of companies, one way or another, globalization is not optional. The companies that thrive will be those that integrate internationalization into their digital strategies from the start.

Practical Case: Mrs. Sarah's Shop

To make this tangible, let's look at a simple case.

Mrs. Sarah owns Good Clothes, a small clothing shop on a side street in Porto. For years, her sales came through word of mouth, and she never worried much about marketing. She opened a Facebook and Instagram page, but never invested seriously in them.

Then came 2020. The pandemic shut down her shop for months, and with no digital channel, she had no way to reach her customers.

A friend introduced her to Marco, a digital marketing specialist. Together, they crafted a plan:

1. Build her own digital commerce portal.
2. List clothes on her own e-commerce shop.
3. Expand to marketplaces like Zalando.

4. Optimize her site for Google visibility.

5. Invest in Instagram advertising to reach new audiences.

Almost immediately, Sara had access to more customers. Sales grew. But then came the next problem: international orders. Shipping with DHL was too costly; she lost money on every cross-border sale.

Marco researched and found a Logistics-as-a-Service provider that charged just one euro per order plus a small storage fee. Suddenly, Sara had global logistics at scale, at a price she could afford.

What changed? Nothing about her core business. She still sold the same clothes, in the same shop. But with digital platforms, she accessed new demand, extended her market internationally, and turned a local boutique into a global seller.

Sara's case illustrates a powerful truth: The digital services economy and globalization are intertwined. With the right platforms, even the smallest company can internationalize without large upfront investment. But this potential often goes unrealized, because as I've said before: "We don't know what we don't know."

Too many leaders simply lack the information. They do not know what digital services exist, what platforms can support them, or how affordable globalization has become. Many stumble upon it by accident, as Sara did through Marco. Ignorance here is not bliss—it is risk.

Shifting the Value Chain

As more services become accessible "as-a-service," companies can reconfigure their value chains. Logistics, marketing, IT infrastructure, payments, and even HR can be outsourced to platforms that offer scale at low cost. This frees smaller firms to focus their limited resources on where they truly add value: unique products, distinctive experiences, or specialized services.

Globalization, combined with digitalization, is not about doing everything yourself. It is about orchestrating partnerships and platforms intelligently.

The Risk of Inaction

Of course, not all companies will seize this opportunity. Many remain anchored in old models, believing their market is "local" or that globalization is for multinationals. But physical barriers are vanishing, and digital platforms are reducing costs and risks. The risk is no longer in trying to expand—it is in not expanding.

Travel agencies illustrate this point. For years, they thrived as intermediaries. Then Booking.com, Skyscanner, and Trivago emerged. Suddenly, customers could compare flights and hotels themselves. Agencies lost their mainstream role. They still exist, but now they serve only a niche of customers who want a managed, high-touch experience. Unless they reinvent themselves—perhaps by integrating with platforms and adding complementary services—their role will continue to shrink.

The same logic applies to almost every industry. Those who ignore the potential of globalization will find themselves competing with companies that embraced it early, and the gap will be hard to close.

Final Thoughts

Globalization, accelerated by digitalization, is one of the most transformative forces in business today. It represents not just a possibility but a necessity. With digital platforms lowering the barriers to entry, companies can access global markets with unprecedented ease.

But this requires awareness, strategy, and action. Leaders must ask:

- Where does our true value lie?
- Which parts of the value chain can we outsource to digital platforms?
- How can we design our strategy for internationalization from the start?

In the near future, I believe more and more companies, as we discussed in previous chapters, will restructure their value chains around digital services and global platforms, focusing their energy on specialization and customer value. For those willing to act, globalization is not a threat—it is the greatest opportunity of our time.

Digital Commerce (E-Commerce)

The 2020 pandemic has changed the way we understand commerce. While we already had a clear trend toward the growth of digital commerce, in the postpandemic era it very quickly became the channel of choice for most consumers.

In a study carried out by Caixa Bank in 2021,[23] it was concluded that in that year Portugal saw a 45 percent increase in the number of people buying via digital commerce. A good indicator is also the fact that 62 percent of companies in 2020 will have a website, which is a good first step.

In 2020, the percentage of digital shoppers in Portugal, my home country, was estimated at 56 percent,[24] while in countries like the United Kingdom the percentage was 92 percent, or 91 percent in the Netherlands. Portugal ranked 27th out of the 37 countries analyzed.

Why has this type of business model grown so much? Because of its convenience.

We have companies like Amazon, which has become a global monster in terms of digital commerce.

In 2024, Amazon surpassed Walmart in revenue in a quarter[25] for the first time ever, Anyone who follows the American economy knows that Walmart is a dinosaur in the industry and just the thought of a completely digital retailer that is in the process of overtaking it is enough to understand the scale of the paradigm shift we are witnessing.

The FBA model, which allows producers to place their products close to consumers, has changed the paradigm of the distribution industry. Today, 24 hours to receive an order is something we expect for most relevant products. The market quickly developed to same-day deliveries. The convenience of going to a shop and trying it on the spot is long gone.

---

[23]"E-Commerce in Portugal During the Pandemic: A Buffer for the Fall in Consumption?" *CaixaBank Research*, October 18, 2021, accessed August 31, 2025, https://www.caixabankresearch.com/en/economics-markets/recent-developments/e-commerce-portugal-during-pandemic-buffer-fall-consumption.

[24]"2021 European E-Commerce Report (Light Version)" *Ecommerce Europe and /EuroCommerce*, September 2021, accessed August 31, 2025, https://ecommerce-europe.eu/publication/2021-european-e-commerce-report-light-version/.

[25]"Amazon Takes Walmart's Revenue Crown (For Now)," *Investor's Business Daily,* February 20, 2025, accessed August 31, 2025.

Companies are already betting on models similar to Amazon's FBA, because it allows them to combat the American giant in delivery services … but it's a very difficult market. In China, Alibaba has its own holiday, Single's day or Double 11, which takes place on November 11 every year.

In 2009, Daniel Zhang, Alibaba's CEO, started using this holiday as a dedicated day (24 hours) for digital commerce, with big discounts. Today, it is the biggest shopping day in the world, for both physical and digital purchases.

Adidas, the historic German clothing brand, which has a turnover of more than 24 billion euros, in 2024,[26] saw in 2020 the majority of its shops close and had to quickly accelerate its digital journey. Since 2020, the company has seen a steady growth of digital business, despite market challenges, having more than 5 billion euros sales reported in 2024. A company that took a chance on its own channel (adidas.com) and has clearly been winning the bet, with a very healthy balance of own channels and wholesale channels.

Alibaba, Amazon and Adidas are three examples of big brands that are at full speed maximizing digital, and this means that many of their consumers, because they use them as a reference, expect the same from any other smaller company. Whether in B2C or B2B. The person who represents a B2B customer is a "C" (consumer) of some other product on a consumer platform. That's why B2B increasingly tends to follow what is done in the B2C market, as the "users" are often the same, but in different roles. When they go to Amazon, they go for their own consumption. When they go to a supplier's website, they go on behalf of the company they work for. Two different moments, but the same person, who therefore can't switch off and have two completely different expectations. They may not expect to find an Amazon, but they will unconsciously demand more from any other company that they would, without those references.

There is no turning back. Investing in digital commerce is no longer optional, and it can cost a company its survival if it doesn't do so. I gave an example of a company that ended up going bankrupt because it resisted this change. We also have the example of Mrs. Sarah, who ended up creating her own digital shop and using a digital marketplace.

---

[26]"Annual Report 2024," Digital Report, *Adidas Group* accessed August 31, 2025, https://report.adidas-group.com/2024/en/.

In the previous chapter, when we talked about the role of globalization (and even earlier in the chapter on the digital service economy), we touched on the fact that companies have a range of services at their disposal that allow them to internationalize much more quickly. Digital commerce is just that—a gateway to a potentially global market.

In one of the first examples in the book, we mentioned the shoe shop that had its market limited to a small location and a few people passing by on the street where the shop is located. This is perhaps the reality of many small shops across the country. Without thinking about digital transformation, that shop's market has no room for growth, because the birth rate isn't so high that thousands of shoe shoppers can be found in a small village somewhere. However, when we expand that physical shop into a digital shop, the potential number of customers becomes almost incalculable, at least in potential. Millions upon millions of people use the Internet on a daily basis, and potentially millions could buy shoes through the shop, provided they know about it and want to.

However, it's not all roses. If it were that easy, any company would create a digital commerce platform for its product and have the problem solved.

Transforming a company for digital commerce, as we've already mentioned, means understanding what customers want and positioning the product in such a way that the customer thinks it's better than the competitor's product. In other words, if a good shoe and a friendly sales assistant were enough in a physical shop on the high street, when you enter the digital world, you're competing with thousands or millions of other possible shops that potentially sell the same thing. Why buy from our shop and our product? If you remember the questions to be answered during a strategy design process, then it becomes even clearer that they don't only apply to large companies. They also apply to the shoe shop that sells on your street and now also sells on the Internet, and with that comes another dimension of demand.

While many small businesses can survive without much of a strategy when they work in physical sales mode, it's much more difficult to do so when you go digital, precisely because your competitor has put more effort into defining their product, their campaigns, their website, photos of their shoes, customer testimonials, and so on.

It's not enough to have a website and a digital shop. You have to think like a bigger company, even if it's just two people.

One of the examples I really like is the Netflix series *La Casa de Papel* (*Money Heist*). It was a huge success on the video platform, but in reality it wasn't created for Netflix. It was created, like so many others, for national channels, and in this case it didn't even have a major impact in Spain. A series in Spanish—without much impact in Spain—would probably be condemned to oblivion. Until one day, Netflix decides to buy the rights and make the series available to its subscribers, perhaps more than 200 million. While Spain has a population of 40/45 million, with many not even being a target audience. In Netflix's case, it's 200 million, all willing to watch content. *La Casa de Papel* went from their "street" to the Internet. What happened next is historic. The *La Casa de Papel* brand with the Salvador Dalí masks became an icon on a global scale. The first and second seasons, which were recorded on a more limited budget, were transferred to Netflix and 10 to 15 million euros were spent on season 5 alone. Another dimension. It can also happen with a shoe shop. If one day there's a shoe that gets into the good graces of an Instagram influencer, it can quickly become the "Money Heist" of shoe sales, and the problem is that if the company doesn't have any thought about what scaling means, it runs the risk of it backfiring, that is, a wave of possible new customers can mean the brand sinking, due to the inability to respond to that demand.

As I talk to entrepreneurs, I realize that many don't fully understand the risk of a digital presence without a more or less defined plan. Some create this presence in order to "be there and then we'll see." And it's that "then we'll see" that can mean losing business. Digital commerce is incredible, but it shouldn't be underestimated because of the volume it can generate. We must remember that failing to fulfill a promise or service can cost more than not having the customer at all.

Lastly, we usually associate digital commerce with the digital shop and the fact that companies sell their products in their shop. That's true, but that's not all.

I therefore want to double click two other concepts in this domain:

1. Digital commerce platforms/digital product marketplaces
2. Social media commerce and the phenomenon of influencers

Digital Commerce Platforms/Electronic Product Marketplaces

The pandemic of 2020 did not invent digital commerce—but it accelerated it to levels that few could have predicted. If e-commerce was already a clear global trend before COVID-19, it became, in the aftermath, the channel of choice for many consumers.

A study by CaixaBank[27] found that just in my home country saw a 45 percent increase in digital buyers in a single year. At the same time, 62 percent of companies had a website, a modest but necessary first step. In 2020, 56 percent[28] of Portuguese consumers shopped online. Compare that with 92 percent in the UK or 91 percent in the Netherlands, and Portugal ranked only 27th out of 37 countries studied. The gap was obvious—but so was the opportunity.

We already brought the examples of adidas, Alibaba or amazon, and how their growth raises the consequence that whether B2C or B2B, consumers now carry the expectations formed by companies like those into every other buying experience. A buyer at a B2B firm is still the same person who shops on Amazon at night. They expect speed, transparency, and ease of use—even if subconsciously.

For many companies, digital commerce is no longer optional. It is survival.

I've seen companies resist and collapse, unwilling to adapt. I've also seen the opposite—like Mrs. Sarah's clothing shop in Porto, which leveraged marketplaces and logistics-as-a-service to internationalize almost overnight.

A shoe shop on a small Portuguese street may only serve a few hundred locals. But online, its potential customer base is in the millions. The Internet breaks the limits of geography—but it also multiplies competition. If in a physical shop "a good product and a friendly salesperson" might suffice, online you compete against thousands of shops selling similar shoes, each optimized with professional photos, influencer campaigns, customer reviews, and polished websites.

That is why strategy matters more in digital than in physical retail. It is not enough to "just be online."

---

[27]"E-Commerce in Portugal During the Pandemic."
[28]"2021 European E-Commerce Report (Light Version)."

Digital commerce is also broader than just having own online store. Growing up, many of us went with our parents to Saturday street markets. Dozens of vendors side by side, shouting prices, offering discounts, competing for attention. Digital marketplaces are their modern twin:

- Multiple suppliers in one place
- Easy comparison of price, features, and delivery
- A single platform that reduces search friction for the customer

Amazon, eBay, Zalando, Etsy, Mercado Libre, Shopee—the list grows every year.

However, when it comes to SMEs, marketplaces are double-edged swords:

- Pro: Instant access to massive demand, minimal setup, built-in trust
- Con: Extreme competition, fee structures that eat margins, and little control over brand experience

Like street markets, marketplaces reward those who stand out—not by shouting louder, but through better positioning, reviews, and digital marketing. Simply listing products is not enough; you must persuade buyers to choose yours.

Social Media Commerce and the Phenomenon of Influencers

When I first joined Instagram years ago, it was for the photography. Beautiful landscapes, food, travel—a place for visual inspiration. What I didn't realize at the time was that I was stepping into what would soon become one of the most powerful commercial engines of our era.

Today, Instagram, TikTok, YouTube, and other social platforms are no longer just about sharing moments—they are marketplaces. The rise of social commerce has reshaped the way products are discovered, marketed, and sold.

What makes social commerce so powerful is the rise of the influencer economy.

In the past, large brands like Coca-Cola, L'Oréal, or Nike relied on celebrities and glossy TV ads. They still do—but now they also rely heavily on influencers: individuals who, through content creation, build trust and loyalty with hundreds of thousands or even millions of followers.

The difference is subtle but important:

- A celebrity is admired for achievements outside the product (sports, film, music).
- An influencer is admired for content creation itself—and the relationship feels more personal, more authentic, more "like us."

This authenticity makes influencer-driven marketing incredibly persuasive. An influencer's audience doesn't just see a product; they see someone they trust using and endorsing it in their daily life.

From Mrs. Sarah's Boutique to Global Attention

Let's return briefly to *Mrs. Sarah's clothing shop* in Porto. Imagine if her friend's daughter had 500,000 Instagram followers. A single post featuring one of Sara's dresses, tagged with the shop's name, could generate a wave of new visitors overnight.

Sometimes this happens by accident—a product is noticed, worn, or mentioned by an influencer, and it goes viral without planning. Other times, it's intentional—with companies paying influencers, sometimes large sums, to feature their products.

This mechanism has made social media one of the most cost-effective yet potentially explosive channels for any company. The right influencer can put a small business in front of thousands or millions of potential customers instantly. But it's also risky:

- Influencer campaigns can be expensive.
- Not every product "translates" well into social formats.
- A viral spike without operational readiness can overwhelm small companies.

Social Commerce Beyond Influencers

Importantly, social commerce is not just about influencers. Platforms themselves are increasingly embedding native shopping features:

- Instagram Shopping lets customers purchase directly from a post.
- TikTok has rolled out live shopping pilots, integrating entertainment and commerce in real time.
- Facebook Shops and Pinterest Shopping allow products to be tagged, searched, and bought without leaving the app.

Add to this paid digital marketing within these platforms—targeted ads in posts, stories, or reels—and social media becomes not just a branding channel but a fully-fledged commerce engine.

Why Leaders Must Pay Attention

For companies, ignoring social commerce is dangerous. Whether you embrace influencers or simply leverage the native commerce tools, social platforms are where many customers discover first. A product seen on Instagram, TikTok, or YouTube often becomes a product searched for on Google or Amazon.

Social media commerce is rising because it combines visibility, convenience, and trust. And while influencers are a big part of this story, the broader shift is that social networks themselves have become digital shopping malls, where entertainment, discovery, and purchase converge.

The Strategic Impacts of Generative AI

One of the most discussed and perplexing technologies of the past few years is generative AI. Boardrooms discuss it in every strategy meeting, headlines describe it as revolutionary, and employees implement it in their day-to-day work. However, what does it actually mean in terms of strategy?

What It Is

One type of AI that can create things is called generative AI. Instead of merely analyzing data or speculating, it can create original text, images, videos, designs, and even code. One could compare it to an exceptionally intelligent apprentice. It has studied how things are made, read millions of books, and viewed billions of images. These days, it can create something that appears believable when requested, such as a draft business plan, a blog post, a product design, or a marketing slogan.

The technological waves that preceded it are not like this. Repeated tasks were replaced by automation. We were able to determine the likelihood of certain outcomes, like whether a customer would leave, thanks to predictive AI. By creating something new, generative AI goes even farther. It feels so transformative because of that creativity, even if it's generated by a machine.

The most important thing to keep in mind is that this is not magic. It is identifying broad patterns. However, when applied properly, it can be a potent copilot for leaders, increasing innovation, accelerating analysis, and altering the way that organizations deliver value.

Where It Is Currently Gaining Traction

Already, generative AI has permeated daily life:

- Writing e-mails, reports, or presentations in Google Docs or Microsoft Office at work
- Anyone can create marketing materials in just a few minutes with design tools like Canva or Adobe Firefly.
- Instant translations, customized trailers, and automatic dubbing make it simple to locate content from around the globe in the media and entertainment industry.
- Students utilize AI tutors in the classroom to practice their languages, write essays, and summarize articles.
- Chatbots in customer service that can engage in genuine dialogue rather than merely reciting prewritten responses

Additionally, entire industries are experimenting:

- Pharmacology: discovering potential novel compounds in weeks as opposed to years

- Sports: creating tactical models, evaluating athletes, and even forecasting game results
- Journalism: producing initial drafts of sports summaries or financial reports in a matter of seconds

It is already altering how work is done, how goods are manufactured, and how services are provided; it is no longer a futuristic concept.

The true question in leadership is not what technology can accomplish. However, how can it provide us with something unique? Among the most significant applications are:

- Product innovation: AI is capable of creating prototypes, testing concepts in a virtual setting, and even accelerating drug research by proposing novel molecules.
- Engaging customers: creating extensive campaigns, product descriptions, or tailored suggestions
- Decision support: leaders can rapidly test "what if" scenarios using scenario simulations.
- Operations: more accurate demand forecasting, user-friendly training guides, or automatically generated process documentation
- Talent and creativity: eliminating tedious duties to allow employees to concentrate on judgment, empathy, and strategy

These are strategic decisions about where to concentrate, how to stand out, and how to ensure that the organization advances rather than merely following the herd. They are not technology projects.

Let's Bring Back Some of Our Stories

Mr. Francis and his restaurant

For many years, Mr. Francis made decisions about which dishes to make more of, when to order extra ingredients, and how to handle reservations based on his intuition and experience. Even a small restaurant like his could use generative AI to predict demand with remarkable accuracy by combining historical patterns with local data, such as weather, festivals, and sporting events. The system may recommend fewer salads and more substantial soups on a wet evening. It may suggest stockpiling wine and seafood before a local celebration. The effect on strategy? Better margins, less waste, and consistently satisfied customers.

AI has the potential to improve customer satisfaction and reservations in addition to the menu. It could forecast peak hours and suggest staffing changes by examining booking trends. For devoted clients, it might even create customized offers; for instance, it might recommend a special menu to a regular codfish buyer. All of a sudden, Mr. Francis's small eatery retains its neighborhood charm while operating with the sophistication of a major hotel chain.

Mrs. Sarah and her tiny shop

When the pandemic forced Mrs. Sarah's store to go online, she had to learn digital marketing almost overnight. Imagine her using generative AI to create lookbooks for her collections, create sophisticated product descriptions in multiple languages, or tailor entire marketing campaigns to target distinct customer segments. She could even take pictures of products that look good without hiring a pro photographer. She can now do things that used to take teams of experts. The final result? A woman who owns a boutique can make her store look as big and fancy as an international fashion house while still being herself.

She could also use generative AI to help her customers. An AI-powered assistant could answer questions in real time, in multiple languages, and keep the brand's tone. This way, the assistant wouldn't have to keep answering the same questions about size and shipping. This enables her to concentrate on the relational and creative aspects of her business, where her unique style is crucial.

The shoe store owned by Mrs. Joanne and Mr. Edward

Only a few people used to be able to visit this family-run shoe store on its peaceful Portuguese street. Generative AI has the potential to open even more doors than digital commerce did. The store could predict future design trends by looking at fashion feeds from around the world. Customers could virtually "try on" shoes before placing an order thanks to the creation of 3D prototypes. Campaigns could be tailored to target customers in Tokyo, New York, or São Paulo.

This represents a significant change for Mrs. Joanne and Mr. Edward, as their small neighborhood store will now be a part of a global footwear conversation. They could create demand rather than just react to it, moving from reactive survival to proactive innovation.

Things to Think About and Risks

Like all effective tools, leaders need to understand their boundaries:

- Truth and accuracy: Generative AI is capable of producing results that appear authentic but are wholly inaccurate. Leaders are unable to relinquish their decision-making authority.
- Ethics and bias: AI can replicate stereotypes or exclude people because it learns from the data it is given. It is crucial to use it sensibly.
- The differentiation trap: Businesses will all have the same appearance if they use the same tools in the same manner. Utilizing AI with your own data, culture, and customer insights yields the greatest benefits.
- The human element: Although AI is capable of writing messages, it is unable to inspire trust in them. It can create a product, but it is unable to lead a group through change. People's leadership, honesty, and empathy are still highly valued.
- Copyright and regulation: Governments are acting swiftly to restrict the application of AI, particularly in regards to issues like false information, privacy, and intellectual property. Leaders must remain vigilant to avoid legal issues and damage to their reputation.

Final Thoughts

Francisco, Sara, and the shoemakers of this world will not be replaced by generative AI. However, it will provide them with the means to think more expansively, move more quickly, and compete more effectively.

Where to use it in a way that adds value that is difficult for others to imitate is the strategic question, not whether to use it at all.

Future successful companies will be shaped by leaders who view it as a partner rather than a gimmick. Those who don't could become overwhelmed by the clamor.

Ten Tips for Getting Technology Right

Buying software is relatively easy. Making the right technology decisions—those that shape not only the next quarter but the next five years—is far more complex.

This book is not about predicting the next trend in cloud computing, blockchain, or AI. Trends change. What doesn't change are the principles behind good decisions. Technology is one of the four fundamental building blocks of digital transformation, and the way companies approach these decisions will determine whether technology becomes an enabler of strategy or a silent anchor holding them back.

Below are 10 tips I give to companies, from a restaurant to a multinational, so they can use as a compass when making technology choices.

1. **Start with the Customer, Not the Code**
   Every technology decision should begin with a simple question: *Who does this serve, what problem does it solve, and what value does it create?* Too often, companies buy tools because a vendor convinces them it's the "next big thing." But technology without a clear link to customer problem-solving is noise. Whether the "customer" is the person paying for your product, or the internal employee trying to get work done, technology must be designed around them. Otherwise, adoption fails and investment is wasted.

2. **Build Only What Makes You Unique**
   If a technology enables competitive advantage, own it. Create intellectual property (IP). That's what differentiates you. For example, Netflix didn't outsource its recommendation algorithm—it built it, because personalization is core to its edge. On the other hand, payroll? HR? Accounting? These don't win you customers. Don't build

them—buy them. Focus scarce engineering capacity where it makes you irreplaceable.

3. **Choose SaaS and PaaS Before Custom Development**

   If a need is standard in your industry, chances are someone has already solved it better than you can. Don't reinvent the wheel. SaaS and PaaS solutions allow you to deploy quickly, scale easily, and reduce support complexity. For nondifferentiating functions, SaaS should be the default. Save custom development for areas tied to customer value or competitive edge.

4. **Keep Your Technology Landscape Simple**

   Complexity kills speed. The more applications you run, the more integration headaches, duplicated data, and redundant costs you create. Simplify. Standardize. Every extra system is not just another license fee—it's another training curve, another support queue, another opportunity for errors. A simple rule: If two systems overlap more than 60 percent in functionality, keep one and retire the other.

5. **Design for Security from Day One**

   Cybersecurity is not optional, nor is it something only "big companies" should care about. In 2017, Maersk was paralyzed by a cyberattack that took down 50,000 laptops and froze global operations. Losses exceeded €400 million. That's a possible cost of underestimating security if we take that loss as an example. From the smallest bakery to the largest bank, every business is digital. That means every business is vulnerable. Prioritize security architecture, access controls, encryption, and employee awareness. One breach can erase years of brand trust in a day.

6. **Treat Data as Your Strategic Asset**

   Data is the raw material of digital transformation. Collected properly, structured carefully, and analyzed intelligently, it becomes the engine for insights, personalization, and innovation. Think beyond immediate utility. Purchase orders, customer interactions, transaction logs, Google Analytics, market research—all of it can become useful later. AI, predictive analytics, and advanced personalization depend on historical data. Companies that fail to treat data as a strategic asset often discover too late that they've been running blind.

7. **Automate What Humans Shouldn't Do**

   Digital transformation is not about replicating inefficient processes in digital form. It's about redesigning processes for automation wherever possible. If a task is predictable, repetitive, and rules-based, a machine should do it—not because people are replaceable but because people should be freed for judgment, creativity, and value creation. Every hour an employee spends copying data from one system to another is an hour of wasted potential. Automation is efficiency plus empowerment.

8. **Go Web-First, Mobility-Ready**

   Business is no longer tied to a desk. People work from airports, living rooms, cafés, and factory floors. Technology must move with them. Web-first applications ensure mobility, flexibility, and lower dependency on installations. Exceptions exist—for example, high-volume graphics rendering or specialized industrial software—but the default should be "web and mobile first." If employees or customers can't access your system anywhere, anytime, you're already behind.

9. **Harness Generative AI as a Cocreator**

   AI is no longer just about automation. With generative AI, technology can create, not just process. It can draft marketing copy, design user interfaces, analyze customer feedback, and accelerate R&D. It's a partner in ideation, not just execution. But as uncle Ben once said, "with great power comes responsibility." Companies must deploy guardrails:
   - Audit for bias and fairness.
   - Protect customer and employee privacy.
   - Be transparent about where and how AI is used.

   Used wisely, generative AI amplifies human capability. Used recklessly, it erodes trust.

10. **Futureproof with Adaptability**

   The only certainty in technology is change. The systems you choose today should not lock you into tomorrow's dead ends. Choose scalable architectures. Negotiate vendor contracts that allow flexibility. Design integrations with replacement in mind. Think of adaptability as resilience: the ability to pivot when markets, customers, or technologies shift. If your systems can't adapt, your strategy won't either.

Final Thoughts

Technology decisions are not IT issues—they are strategic business choices. They affect customer experience, employee productivity, financial resilience, and long-term competitiveness. By following these 10 principles, companies avoid chasing trends blindly and instead design technology landscapes that are simple, secure, scalable, and centered on value. Digital transformation is not about technology for its own sake. It's about using technology as the enabler of strategy, customer success, and future growth.

Hypothesis-Driven Strategy

It is difficult to predict the future, but it is possible to mitigate this limitation by ensuring that decisions are not made solely on the basis of opinions.

Throughout my career, I have never met anyone who is infallible when it comes to predicting the future. I have met people who are good at assessing possibilities, taking calculated risks, and reading market signals—but *predicting* in the strict sense? That is impossible. The truth is, none of us knows what will happen in the next few seconds, let alone in the next 12 or 24 months. That is precisely what makes defining strategy so difficult: The medium- to long-term horizon is always clouded by uncertainty.

Take COVID-19 as an example. Who, when writing their 2019 business plans, had factored in a global pandemic and the shutdown of economic activity as plausible scenarios for the following year? Probably no one. Even though the risk of pandemics was known, it was not considered relevant enough to be embedded into corporate strategies. And yet, just a few months later, the entire global economy was thrown into crisis. This is why strategies built exclusively on forecasts and assumptions, without mechanisms for testing and adaptation, are so fragile.

This is where the hypothesis-driven approach comes in. I am particularly fond of it when thinking about digital transformation. Transformation is by definition unpredictable—it is an experiment with no guaranteed outcome. Rather than pretending we can plan everything down to the last detail, we should recognize our limitations and structure our strategies as a series of hypotheses to be tested.

The idea is simple: Instead of assuming we know everything, we formulate explicit hypotheses about the decisions we are making, and then design processes to validate or reject those hypotheses through evidence. In this way, we move away from making decisions based on opinion alone, and instead build strategies based on learning loops.

There is plenty of literature that supports this approach. For instance, Jessica Menold et al.'s[29] work describes hypotheses as falling into categories of *desirable*, *doable*, and *feasible*. These categories help companies organize their assumptions, and prioritize what needs testing first.

Think back to the Four-Floor Model we discussed earlier. Each floor—vision, success criteria, problems, and initiatives—is filled with assumptions. When we define a vision, when we decide what results to pursue, or when we select which activities to execute, we are implicitly making bets about what we think will work.

The hypothesis-driven strategy makes those bets explicit. It forces us to say out loud: "I believe that ..." and then to design an experiment to see whether that belief holds true.

Take the example of Mrs. Sarah's clothing shop. When she set up her first online store, she had very little information about how her loyal physical-store customers would react. One possible hypothesis might have been: "I believe that customers who buy in the physical shop, if they receive a letter or e-mail about our new online shop, will shop online with the same frequency as they do in the physical shop."

That single sentence contains an assumption that could make or break the digital strategy. If true, it would mean she could lean on her existing customer base and invest less in marketing to acquire new customers. If false, it would mean her strategy had to shift dramatically, requiring investment in digital advertising, partnerships, or influencer campaigns.

The beauty of a hypothesis is that it can be tested in small, low-risk ways. Mrs. Sarah could select 30 loyal customers, send them an e-mail

---

[29]Jessica Menold, Kathryn W. Jablokow, Timothy W. Simpson, and Emily A. Waterman, "The Prototype for X (PFX) Framework: Assessing Its Impact on Students' Prototyping Awareness," Paper presented at the ASEE Annual Conference & Exposition, New Orleans, June 26–29, 2016.

about the new shop, and measure how many made online purchases. She could do the same with 20 customers using physical letters. If 80 percent of customers engaged and bought online, the hypothesis is validated and she can move forward confidently. If only 10 percent responded, then the hypothesis is disproved—and she avoids scaling a flawed assumption that could have wasted time and money.

The Three Categories of Hypotheses

In practice, I like to organize hypotheses into three broad categories. This not only creates clarity but also prevents an overload of untested assumptions.

1. Desirable—hypotheses about what the customer wants. These cover assumptions about demand, features, price sensitivity, or brand perception.
   Example: "I believe that customers are more likely to buy additional items if we offer free returns on larger purchases."
2. Doable—hypotheses about the company's ability to deliver. These test assumptions about operations, capabilities, and execution capacity.
   Example: "I believe that we can respond to all customer service requests within 24 hours, which will increase customer satisfaction."
3. Feasible—hypotheses about the business's financial and operational viability. These cover assumptions about cost structures, margins, or minimum volumes.
   Example: "I believe that to achieve a 20 percent operating margin, logistics costs must not exceed €2 per unit."

By categorizing hypotheses, we can quickly see where the greatest risks lie. A desirable hypothesis tests whether customers even care about what we are offering. A doable hypothesis tests whether we can actually deliver on the promise. A feasible hypothesis ensures that even if the first two are true, the economics make sense.

The Discipline of Testing

One of the challenges with this approach is scope. If we try to turn every unknown into a hypothesis, we will drown in testing and analysis. That is not the point. The goal is not to eliminate all uncertainty, but to identify the few critical assumptions that carry the highest risk.

Too many hypotheses can create three problems:

- A strategy with too many unvalidated assumptions becomes fragile and unfocused.
- Testing every single hypothesis is operationally impossible.
- Constantly reversing decisions after failed tests creates fatigue and confusion.

That is why prioritization is essential. Focus on the hypotheses that, if wrong, would derail the entire strategy. Focus also on those where there is the least existing data, and therefore the greatest uncertainty.

The format I use is deliberately simple: Write hypotheses as "I believe that …" statements. This makes them easy to communicate, easy to understand, and easy to test.

Take the example: "I believe that reducing the price of this product by 15 percent in northern Germany will increase sales sufficiently to justify the margin loss."

Once written, these hypotheses become the building blocks of the strategy. They are not predictions—they are structured bets. And every bet must be validated with data, feedback, and evidence.

Why This Matters for Digital Transformation

Digital transformation, by its nature, multiplies uncertainty. New technologies, shifting customer behaviors, and global competition make it impossible to design a perfect roadmap in advance. A hypothesis-driven strategy respects this reality. It acknowledges unpredictability and builds adaptability into the plan.

Instead of "betting the farm" on a single grand plan, companies can advance in stages, testing and learning as they go. This approach avoids large investments based on unproven assumptions and ensures that strategy evolves as the environment changes.

Ultimately, a hypothesis-driven strategy is a mindset. It shifts the culture of decision making from one of *certainty* to one of *curiosity*. It forces leaders to be humble enough to admit they don't know everything, but disciplined enough to test, measure, and learn.

As mentioned before, the famous Roger Martin's quote *"Strategy isn't what you say, It's what you do."* Testing hypotheses is how we make sure our doing matches our saying.

In the next part, we will connect this approach back to the broader framework of transformation—because testing assumptions is not just a tool for product development or marketing, but a way to derisk and strengthen the entire digital strategy.

From Hypothesis to Action: Designing and Testing with Discipline

In the context of this book, we are not talking about the scientific model for hypothesis testing. In academia, when we talk about experimentation and validation, there is a rigorous set of rules, protocols, and statistical frameworks that must be followed. That level of precision, while critical in research, is not always practical or necessary in the world of business transformation. Here, the goal is simpler: Test and validate in a way that gives you enough confidence to move forward—knowing full well there will always be a margin of error. Accepting risk is part of being a leader. The purpose of testing in a business transformation context is not perfection but informed decision making. The first choice, therefore, is deciding *how* to test a given hypothesis. Depending on the situation, different approaches may be more appropriate.

Practical Ways to Test a Hypothesis

1. Interviews and questionnaires
   One of the simplest and most widely used techniques. This involves asking customers (or internal stakeholders) targeted questions designed around the hypotheses you want to validate. It can be structured, such as surveys sent to large groups, or more exploratory, such as in-depth interviews. Used properly, this method can reveal

customer habits, behaviors, and preferences that either support or disprove assumptions. It is particularly valuable in market research or early product discovery phases.

2. Prototypes, pilots, AB testing

Sometimes, asking questions is not enough. People often say one thing and do another. In these cases, the best approach is to test behavior in the real world. Creating prototypes, minimum viable products (MVPs), or pilot programs allows companies to validate hypotheses at relatively low cost. By observing how customers interact with these early versions, organizations can collect real evidence about what works, what doesn't, and what needs to change—before making a full investment. Do they react different to option A or option B, how? What do we learn?

3. Analyzing historical data

The past can often be a reliable predictor of future behavior. Companies with a strong data history have a significant advantage, as they can mine this information to test assumptions about demand, costs, seasonality, or customer behavior. For example, if the hypothesis is that free shipping increases average order value, a company can look at past campaigns where shipping was free and compare the results. Historical data doesn't always have all the answers, but it can provide useful signals to confirm or challenge beliefs.

These are three examples, but the principle is broader: Any method that produces usable evidence can be a testing tool. What matters is that leaders feel confident with the data collected and are willing to adapt decisions based on that evidence.

Building a Test Plan

Hypotheses without a plan often lead nowhere. A test plan doesn't have to be complex, but it should capture three essential elements:

What:

- What exactly are we testing?
- What data or evidence will be collected?
- Which hypothesis are we trying to confirm or discard?

When:

- What is the timeline?
- Are we testing for a week, a month, or a defined number of customer interactions?

How and Outcome:

- How will it be analyzed?
- Who is responsible for acting on the result?
- How will the results be displayed

These simple questions keep testing grounded in reality. Every hypothesis should have a test plan that defines the scope, method, and expected outputs. This ensures that testing is actionable rather than theoretical.

Practical Case: Mrs. Sarah's Shop

Let's go back to Mrs. Sarah and her clothing shop. When she launched her new online store, one of her main challenges was to convince loyal physical-shop customers to also buy digitally. She didn't know whether her existing customers would make the switch.

She defined a hypothesis: "I believe that if I send my physical-shop customers a personalized letter with a discount code for their first online purchase, at least 30 percent of them will try the online shop within one month."

Simple test plan:

1. What?
   She will send 50 personalized letters with discount codes.
2. Whan?
   The campaign will run over four weeks, tracking usage of the codes.
3. How and Outcome?
   She will measure the percentage of customers who redeem the codes, and compare purchase frequency and average order value between those who switched and those who didn't.

Possible outcomes:

- If more than 30 percent buy online, the hypothesis is confirmed, and she can reduce marketing spend on new-customer acquisition while focusing on converting existing ones.
- If fewer than 10 percent respond, the hypothesis is disproven, and she knows she must invest more heavily in broader digital marketing to acquire new customers.

This simple, low-cost test gives Mrs. Sarah the evidence she needs to make a critical strategic decision without betting everything blindly.

Linking Testing to the Business Model

This approach aligns naturally with the Business Model Canvas we will show next. Each of the nine blocks of the canvas is full of assumptions, and each assumption can be framed as a hypothesis in one of three categories:

- Desirable: linked to *customer segments, relationships, channels, value proposition*
- Doable: linked to *key activities, key resources, key partners*
- Feasible: linked to cost structure, *revenue streams*

By mapping hypotheses against the canvas, companies can clearly see where the greatest risks lie and where testing should be prioritized.

Why Testing Matters

At its core, this discipline helps leaders mitigate risks and make better-informed decisions. It may seem like a cumbersome process at first, but once it becomes part of the culture, it is straightforward and powerful.

Transformations rarely fail because leaders lack vision. More often, they fail because decisions are made without sufficient validation—based on feelings, assumptions, or internal politics rather than evidence. Leaders act with conviction, but without data.

A hypothesis-driven strategy recognizes the unpredictability of transformation and builds mechanisms to progressively close the gap of ignorance. It accepts that the future cannot be predicted, but it can be *tested into*. Each experiment reduces uncertainty, builds confidence, and moves the organization closer to sustainable transformation.

Models That Support Decision Making

In this chapter, we have dived quite deep in various options that companies can act on, when making decisions in terms of transformation. There are a few additional models that can support in those decisions by providing a structure on how to organize the thoughts and structure the information.

We will deep dive in two:

- Business Model Canvas: a widely used model to describe business models through nine boxes
- Transformation Modeling Canvas: a proprietary model that helps summarizing a lot of the topics we have been discussing through this book; more focused on a transformation, and less on a specific business model

Business Model Canvas

Since the business model is one of the five pillars (FRAME) for digital success, I couldn't fail to address a way of designing (and documenting) different business models. Thinking about a digital strategy also means thinking about how to position the company in order to develop alternative business models, or how to improve the main business models. The model I like to use most is the Business Model Canvas (BMC). This model was first proposed by Osterwalder and Pigneur,[30] and over the years it has become one of the most widely used frameworks in business, precisely because of its simplicity and power. At its core, it proposes that

---

[30]Alexander Osterwalder and Yves Pigneur, *Business Model Generation: A Handbook for Visionaries, Game Changers, and Challengers* (John Wiley & Sons, 2010).

a business model can be described through nine building blocks, with the way these blocks relate to each other defining how the business model works in practice.

Osterwalder defined it very clearly: *"A business model describes the logic of how an organization creates, delivers and captures value."* The power of the BMC is that it transforms this definition into a visual and structured tool that helps us map the different pieces of a company's value chain, customer promise, and economic engine.

The nine blocks are usually grouped under four broad questions that structure the logic of the business:

1. Who?
   Here we identify the *customer segments* we want to serve. Who exactly are the people (or organizations) that will buy from us? We also define the *channels* through which the company delivers value to those customers, and the *type of relationship* we intend to establish. Will it be high-touch and personalized, or fully digital and automated?

2. What?
   This is the *value proposition*: the essence of what the company offers, and why it matters. It is not just "the product," but the problem we are solving for the customer, the job-to-be-done we fulfill, and the reason customers choose us over competitors.

3. How?
   Here we describe the engine of delivery: the *key activities* that must be performed, the *key resources* required, and the *partners* we depend on. This is about the backbone of execution—what we actually need to do and have in place to make the value proposition real for customers.

4. How much?
   Finally, we describe the economics: the cost structure (what it takes to deliver value) and the sources of revenue (how money comes in). This forces us to see if the model is sustainable and scalable.

One of the things I appreciate most about the BMC is how it creates a common language. Too often, conversations about business models are vague or lost in abstraction. By mapping the nine blocks, we are forced to be concrete. And because the model is visual, it allows a management team—or even an entire company—to literally "see" how the business works, spot gaps, and challenge assumptions.

This framework has also been validated in research. In a 2020 study, Fika Fitriasari[31] analyzed how SMEs responded to the COVID-19 pandemic and the challenges they faced in building resilience during such an uncertain time. The author used the Business Model Canvas as a way of analyzing alternative models, demonstrating its value as a practical tool to explore new strategic possibilities in the midst of disruption.

For me, the lesson is clear: Whether we are talking about a small family-owned business or a global corporation, the Canvas is a tool that helps leaders clarify, align, and document the underlying logic of their business. It also serves as a living document: It should not only be completed once, at the end of a strategic process, but should be revisited, refined, and updated as we move forward. Even in draft form, it is immensely valuable because it records the assumptions we are making about customers, value, operations, and revenue.

Practical Case: Fresh Paintings

To make this more tangible, let's take a fictional but realistic company: *Fresh Paintings*. The company specializes in artistic wall paintings for homes. For years, the business was run in a traditional way: Bookings were made over the phone, painters were dispatched, and everything was managed manually.

As digitalization gained momentum, the founders decided they needed to rethink their model. They wanted to expand their reach, modernize the customer experience, and create more scalable ways of delivering their service. The idea they came up with was to create a digital platform: a space where clients could book painters online, upload their own designs, access external designers for inspiration, and even connect with freelance painters in cases where Fresh Paintings' own team wasn't available.

---

[31]Fika Fitriasari, "How Do Small and Medium Enterprises (SMEs) Survive the COVID-19 Outbreak?" *Jurnal Inovasi Ekonomi* 5, no. 2 (2020): 53–62.

In BMC terms, their value proposition was clear: *bringing unique, personalized art into people's homes in a simple, convenient, and professional way.*

Their customer segments were art-loving individuals with disposable income—young singles in their 30s and 40s, homeowners looking to personalize their spaces, and families willing to invest in aesthetic home improvements. These customers would be reached through channels such as Google searches, social media, and targeted advertising campaigns. The relationship would be managed primarily through the platform, with telephone support available only when needed.

Delivering on this promise required several key activities:

- Providing the painting service itself
- Validating customer-uploaded designs
- Running a service marketplace where external painters could bid on jobs
- Managing customer bookings, payments, and satisfaction

To do this, the company relied on key resources: its own team of painters, a network of external painters, the digital platform, and a customer support service. It also needed partners, particularly suppliers of painting materials who could ensure quality and reliability.

From a financial standpoint, the cost structure included the development and maintenance of the digital platform, materials, salaries for painters and customer service staff, and the fees paid to external painters. The revenue streams came from direct painting services, upsells like premium designs or maintenance packages, and transaction commissions from external painters using the marketplace.

By mapping out their business in this way, Fresh Paintings could see very clearly where the model created value and where the costs lay. More importantly, it provided them with a framework to test viability: If their cost base was €10 per service, but their expected revenue was only €5, then something had to change. Conversely, if the economics worked, they had a model worth scaling.

Why This Matters

The Fresh Paintings example is simple, but it illustrates why the Business Model Canvas is such a powerful tool in digital transformation. It forces leaders to articulate how their business actually works and to see the interconnections between customers, operations, resources, and financials.

In practice, the BMC also aligns well with other models we've covered, such as the Four-Floor Model. While the Four Floors help move from vision to execution, the BMC provides the structural "map" of how the business is supposed to generate value in the first place. When combined, these tools give leaders a much clearer path from ambition to action.

Ultimately, business models are the foundation of digital transformation. Without a clear model that explains how value is created, delivered, and captured, any technological investment or customer initiative is built on sand. The Business Model Canvas gives us the language, the framework, and the discipline to avoid that mistake.

In the next chapter, we'll look at the hypothesis-driven strategy, a natural complement to the BMC, which helps test and validate the assumptions embedded in any business model before scaling it too far.

Transformation Modeling Canvas

Throughout the chapter on strategies, we've covered a wide set of techniques, principles, and potential strategic concepts that can guide a company in transforming itself into a digital business. We have spoken about vision, business models, digital commerce, globalization, technology decisions, hypothesis-driven strategy, and disruptive approaches like digital twins or generative AI. Each of these topics is important in isolation, but their real power only emerges when they are connected into a coherent whole.

The most common challenge I see in organizations is not the lack of frameworks, but the inability to tie all the different pieces together into a clear strategy that can be executed. It is one thing to analyze the customer journey, document hypotheses, or explore alternative business models. It is another thing entirely to integrate these insights into a structured plan that moves the company forward.

This is where discipline and structure are essential. There is no universal formula that guarantees success, but there are ways of working that increase the likelihood of making better decisions. Thinking in a structured way helps leaders avoid blind spots, make priorities visible, and ensure that action is anchored in both external reality and internal capability.

At this stage, a company should have collected several building blocks:

- A set of data and insights about its customers—who they are, what problems they face, what they value, and how they behave
- A clear internal analysis of the organization's strengths and weaknesses—the SWOT, but also the capabilities and constraints that shape what is possible
- A definition of the company's competitive advantage—the "right to win" that distinguishes it from others in the market
- A set of strategic themes and options, such as internationalization, automation, or digital commerce, which need to be prioritized
- A hypothesis plan that makes assumptions explicit and defines how they will be tested

This is a lot of information. Leaders often struggle at this point: They have fragments of analysis and insights but lack a way to assemble them into a strategy that can guide execution.

To help with this integration, I developed the ASCEND Modeling Canvas (as illustrated in Fig 7.1), which brings together the different elements into one coherent picture. The canvas is not another abstract framework but rather a simple boxed visualization of the blocks to expect across all these phases.

Using the ASCEND Modeling Canvas

The canvas has several sections, each of which connects to the content we have discussed in this chapter:

1. Internal Perspective (Company): It reflects the company's strengths, weaknesses, resources, and constraints. It forces realism and prevents strategies from being designed in isolation from organizational reality. No matter how ambitious the vision, transformation must start by knowing what you have and where you are today.

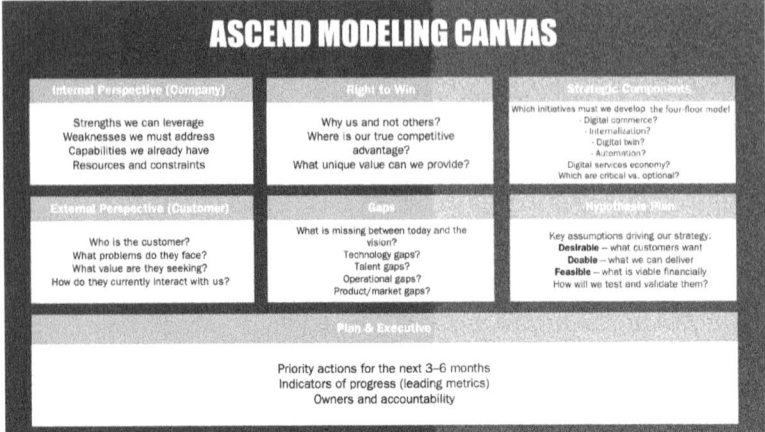

Figure 7.1 ASCEND Modeling Canvas

2. External Perspective (Customer): Once we have clarity on the internal side, we turn outward. This captures who the customer is, what problems they face, what value they are seeking, and how they currently interact with the company. Without this, any digital initiative risks being technology for technology's sake.

3. Right to Win: This is the critical bridge between external and internal. Why us and not others? What is our unique competitive advantage? What value can we provide that competitors cannot easily replicate? This question forces companies to sharpen their positioning.

4. Gaps: Here the focus is on what is missing between today and the desired future. Technology gaps, talent gaps, operational gaps, product gaps—by naming them explicitly, we avoid assuming that ambition will automatically translate into reality.

5. Strategic Components: This box captures the initiatives that must be developed to close those gaps. Throughout this chapter, we mentioned some examples: digital commerce, internationalization, digital twins, automation, the digital services economy. Each organization must identify which are critical, which are optional, and how they interrelate.

6. Hypothesis Plan: Every strategy is based on assumptions, whether about customer desirability, operational *doability*, or financial

feasibility. Making these assumptions visible and testable is what transforms strategy from opinion into evidence-based learning.

7. Plan and Execution: Finally, all of this converges into tangible next steps: priority actions for the next three to six months, indicators of progress (leading metrics), and owners who are accountable. Without this final box, even the best strategy remains only a document.

Why It Matters

The ASCEND Modeling Canvas is valuable because it allows leaders to integrate all the insights we have explored into one structured view. It does not replace tools like the Business Model Canvas or the Four-Floor Model—instead, it complements them by serving as the integrative layer where everything comes together.

What makes this approach powerful is that it forces companies to work through the logic of transformation systematically:

1. Start with the internal perspective—the company's reality.
2. Balance it the external perspective—the customer.
3. Define the right to win—the unique advantage.
4. Identify the gaps that block progress.
5. Select the strategic components that must be developed.
6. Make assumptions explicit in the hypothesis plan.
7. Translate all of this into a plan for execution.

In other words, it takes the many ideas we have discussed—from vision design to disruptive models—and ensures they are not left as theory but transformed into a plan of action.

Digital transformation fails when strategies stay abstract or fragmented. The ASCEND Modeling Canvas closes the gap by offering leaders a way to synthesize complexity into clarity, and clarity into execution. It provides a disciplined bridge between analysis and action, ensuring that what the company *knows* is directly connected to what the company *does*.

PART 4

Building on Decisions and Make It Last

Executing with Structure and Intent to Last

Decisions only matter if they become results. This part builds the structures, processes, and rhythms that carry choices into delivery—and keep them there.

We've been talking about various aspects of this whole transformation journey, starting with understanding what it means to transform, moving on to the company, the customer and the different strategies for tackling the problems that customers are looking for solutions to. All of these processes make it possible to generate content, information and data so that it can be put into practice, creating an execution plan that must be managed in an exemplary manner if the transformation is to be successful.

If designing a digital transformation is challenging, trust me, executing is much harder. Up to this point, we've explored vision, strategy, customers, technology, and new business models. We've used frameworks such as the Four-Floor Model, the Business Model Canvas, and hypothesis-driven strategy to define what and *why* of transformation. But the truth is simple: Nothing matters until it is executed.

Many companies fail at this exact stage. They spend months (or years) in workshops, presentations, and strategies, but stumble when turning ideas into outcomes. Plans get lost in PowerPoint slides, resources are stretched thin, and initiatives lack coordination. Some even confuse "starting" with "executing"—launching pilots without the structures needed to scale.

This chapter is about avoiding that trap.

CHAPTER 8

The SCRIPT Framework

I propose the SCRIPT framework to structure execution. SCRIPT is not about *redefining vision* or *choosing strategy*. Those were earlier steps. SCRIPT assumes that the company already has a defined scope, a clear strategy, and a vision agreed upon. SCRIPT is about making it happen.

SCRIPT brings discipline to execution—clarifying scope, securing capabilities, planning the route, delivering in increments, and maintaining momentum and learning through progress and tracking.

It follows five logical workflows:

Scope: Confirm and operationalize the agreed scope of transformation.
Capital and Capabilities: Ensure resources, skills, and readiness are in place.
Roadmap: Translate vision into a sequence of actionable steps.
Implementation: Execute with discipline and adapt quickly.
Progress: Monitor progress
Tracking: Measure and adjust.

Think of SCRIPT as the engine room of transformation. If earlier chapters gave us the design of the ship, SCRIPT is how we get it moving, adjusting sails when the wind changes, and ensuring the crew rows in the same direction.

S—Scope: Confirming the Playing Field

Scope defines the boundaries of execution. It is not about setting strategy—that work has already been done through analysis models such as the Four Floors. Instead, scope is about *making strategy clear*: translating intent into concrete focus areas, deliverables, and limits. Without clear scope, even the best plans drift.

Practical Case: The Insurance Company

A midsize insurance company decided, at the strategy level, that their transformation focus would be digital self-service for customers. At the execution stage, defining scope meant translating this into tangible choices:

- Which processes will be digitalized first (claims versus policy issuance)?
- Which markets will go first (domestic before international)?
- Which KPIs define success (e.g., 60 percent of claims submitted digitally within 12 months)?

Scope is about:

- Translating strategic intent into specific, measurable deliverables
- Defining what is inside and outside the transformation program
- Aligning stakeholders on priorities to prevent scope creep and resource waste
- Setting clear success criteria before execution begins

Scope is ultimately about **focus**—confirming the playing field so everyone knows where the game is being played, and what winning looks like.

Clear scope defines the game; now we need the means to play it. Capital and capabilities ensure ambition is matched with the people, budget, and technology to deliver.

C—Capital and Capabilities: Resourcing for Success

A strategy without resources is just a wish. Capital and capabilities turn intention into feasibility—ensuring the organization has the people, skills, funding, and technology to make execution possible.

Practical Case: The Retail Company

A retail chain decided to launch an e-commerce platform. The business case was solid, but when execution began, the team discovered critical gaps: no in-house UX designers, weak cybersecurity, and an IT budget already 30 percent overrun. The initiative stalled before it started.

Capital and capabilities is about:

- Ringfencing financial resources and protecting them from competing priorities.
- Identifying required skills early—train, hire, or partner.
- Ensuring technology foundations (infrastructure, data, and security) are robust.
- Embedding change management from the outset—employees must be prepared, not surprised.

This step asks a simple but defining question: *Do we truly have what it takes to execute?*

With resources aligned, planning becomes sequencing: what happens first, what depends on what, and how momentum is built wave by wave.

R—Roadmap: Planning the Path Forward

Once resources are secured, execution must be structured. A roadmap is more than a timeline—it's a deliberate sequence of priorities that connects ambition to delivery. It defines *what happens first, what depends on what,* and *how success will unfold over time.*

Practical Case: The Health Care Provider

A health care provider wanted to introduce telemedicine. Instead of building everything at once, their roadmap broke the journey into waves:

- Pilot consultations in one region.
- Expand to chronic patients nationwide.
- Integrate wearables and data-driven care.

By structuring initiatives this way, the organization ensured that progress was cumulative—each wave built capability and confidence for the next. A well-designed roadmap keeps focus clear, respects dependencies, and delivers visible results. Without it, companies try to "boil the ocean," and progress collapses under its own weight.

A roadmap is about:

- Translating ambition into a sequenced, achievable plan
- Defining dependencies, milestones, and ownership
- Balancing speed with learning—scaling only what works
- Making strategy visible, so everyone understands the journey ahead

Plans earn their value in delivery. Implementation turns choices into visible progress across teams and processes.

I—Implementation: Turning Plans into Action

Implementation is where strategy becomes visible—projects are delivered, systems go live, and new processes take shape. It's the phase that tests both planning and leadership, translating ideas into tangible results.

Practical Case: The Furniture Manufacturer

A furniture manufacturer introduced a WMS. Rather than launching it nationwide, they began with a single distribution center, refining the system based on employee feedback before scaling it across the network. This phased approach built confidence, minimized risk, and accelerated learning.

Implementation is about:

- Delivering in small, testable increments that enable agility and adaptation
- Maintaining cross-functional collaboration—digital transformation rarely belongs to one department

- Supporting employees through intentional change management and communication
- Using governance and ownership structures to ensure account- ability and avoid duplication

Progress is cadence and momentum—making work visible, decisions timely, and teams aligned around milestones.

P—Progress: Monitoring Momentum and Milestones

Progress is about rhythm. It ensures that execution doesn't lose energy be- tween kickoff and completion. Whereas Tracking focuses on measurement and learning, Progress is about maintaining visibility, pace, and accountabil- ity as work unfolds. Transformation often fails not because of poor strategy but because momentum fades and small delays compound into inertia.

Practical Case: The Retail Group

A retail group launched a new digital loyalty platform with a 12-month rollout plan. By introducing biweekly progress reviews, visible milestone charts, and quick-decision routines, the leadership team kept energy high and decisions fast. The cadence itself became a source of alignment— problems were surfaced early, and wins were shared broadly. The initiative delivered on time, with 15 percent higher engagement than projected.

Progress is about:

- Visible milestones and deliverables that mark tangible advancement
- Routines and cadences that keep teams aligned (e.g., weekly stand-ups, steering reviews)
- Celebrating small wins to sustain motivation
- Early detection of slippage or overload before it escalates

If progress keeps us moving, tracking keeps us honest—measuring outcomes, learning from evidence, and adjusting course before small drifts become big detours.

T—Tracking: Measuring and Adapting

Execution is never "set and forget." Tracking ensures that transformation stays on course and that decisions remain grounded in evidence. It's where data meets learning.

Practical Case: A Logistics Company

A logistics company digitalized its delivery booking system. The target was a 30 percent increase in self-service bookings within 12 months. Tracking revealed only 10 percent adoption after six months. Instead of calling it failure, the company adjusted—running customer-education campaigns and improving the interface. Adoption then jumped to 28 percent.

Tracking is about:

- Clear KPIs and OKRs defined upfront
- Real-time dashboards and visibility
- Feedback loops from employees and customers
- A willingness to adapt or pivot when results don't match assumptions

---

Keeping SCRIPT Together with Governance

Without governance, SCRIPT unravels. Execution becomes chaos when there's no coordination or accountability.

We recommend a dual-level governance model:

- For large corporations: a central steering committee, workflow leaders for each SCRIPT phase, and a program office to track KPIs and interdependencies
- For SMEs: a single transformation lead, a lean cross-functional team, and light-touch steering, with external partners filling skill gaps

Governance is the invisible glue of SCRIPT. It ensures decisions are made, issues escalated, and initiatives remain connected to strategy.

Final Thoughts

Execution is the hardest part of digital transformation—not because leaders lack ideas but because they underestimate the discipline needed to move from vision to reality. SCRIPT provides that discipline. It connects earlier strategy work (vision, Four Floors, customer focus, technology decisions) with the practical engine of delivery. It ensures resources are aligned, priorities sequenced, execution supported, and progress measured.

Above all, SCRIPT reminds us that transformation is not just about starting projects—it's about finishing them, learning from them, and scaling them until they reshape the company's DNA.

CHAPTER 9

Behavioral Change

Technology can be bought. Processes can be redesigned. But people—their habits, beliefs, motivations, and fears—are infinitely more complex. For every digital transformation project that fails, the common denominator is rarely just the wrong software or flawed strategy. More often, it is the failure to change behaviors at scale.

Behavioral change is influenced by multiple forces:

1. Cognitive (what I know)
2. Emotional (what I feel)
3. Social (what others expect of me)
4. Structural (what systems make easier or harder)

Leaders often underestimate how strongly these dimensions interact. Announcing new behaviors is not enough; humans are not machines waiting for updated instructions. They are meaning-seeking beings, shaped by identity, context, and motivation.

This chapter explores how organizations can influence, enable, and sustain behavioral adoption by combining three models:

1. McKinsey's Influence Model[32]
2. The ENRICH model (proprietary framework)
3. The Leadership CORE5 model (proprietary framework)

Together, they form a strong set of support tools that can help organizations move from awareness to adoption to authentic leadership-led reinforcement.

---

[32]Tessa Basford and Bill Schaninger, "The Four Building Blocks of Change," *McKinsey Quarterly*, April 11, 2016, accessed September 2, 2025, https://www. mckinsey.com/capabilities/people-and-organizational-performance/our-insights/ the-four-building-blocks--of-change

McKinsey's Influence Model

For many years, corporate change initiatives have made extensive use of McKinsey & Company's Influence Model, which breaks down behavioral adoption into four levers. Its strength comes from acknowledging that people rarely change for a single reason; instead, they require several reminders.

The Four Levers

1. Promoting Conviction and Understanding: People must understand the significance of change. Both the heart (meaning) and the head (logic) must be connected in communication. As an illustration, a bank that digitalized onboarding convinced customers that the new systems would reduce wait times by 40 percent, going above and beyond cost savings.
2. Reinforcing with Formal Mechanisms: The new behavior needs to be rewarded by processes, metrics, and incentives. When a behavior is ignored or punished, people stop doing it. For instance, a telecom company implemented KPIs pertaining to the adoption of digital channels. Bonuses were not given to managers unless adoption goals were reached.
3. Developing Talent and Skills: Individuals don't change until they believe they can. Even with intent, adoption is impeded by skills gaps. For instance, until employees received practical training in their mother tongues, a logistics company did not implement a warehouse app.
4. Role Modeling: Leaders need to exhibit the behaviors they want to see. Leadership hypocrisy sabotages change more quickly than anything else. For instance, executives at a multinational retailer openly switched to utilizing the digital HR portal exclusively. Staff adoption came shortly after.

Practical Case: Insurance Call Centers

AI-assisted claim triage was implemented by an insurer. Before the four levers were pulled, adoption stalled: Managers used the tool themselves, formal KPIs measured digital claims, training increased confidence, and leaders explained the "why" (faster payouts for distressed customers). Digital-first processing became commonplace in a matter of months.

The ENRICH Framework

The ENRICH framework is a proprietary approach for guiding behavioral evolution during transformation. It reframes change not as "compliance" but as growth and enrichment—for individuals, teams, and organizations. Each stage builds a psychological foundation that turns awareness into sustainable adoption.

Engage—Building Awareness with Meaning

The first thing to do is get involved. People don't change just because we give them a new manual or tell them it's important. They change when they understand why, both emotionally and intellectually. This stage is about helping workers understand why we need certain behaviors and how they fit together.

The psychology of change has been pointing this way for a long time. Kurt Lewin's Change Theory[33] said that people need to "unfreeze" from their current patterns before any new behaviors can stick. John Kotter[34] made the same point almost 50 years later when he said that the first step to leading change is to make people feel like they need to act quickly. People just don't get involved if there isn't a sense of urgency or relevance.

A European store that installs a digital point-of-sale system is a good example. Management could have told people, "Please learn this new software." Instead, they talked about how the system would make things easier for staff: "This cuts checkout time by 40%, which means fewer angry customers, fewer returns, and more energy for you." What could have felt like just another thing to learn turned out to be something that made a daily problem go away. People didn't get involved with the system itself; they got involved by connecting it to real problems that employees were having.

When you think about how you want to change, it's a good idea to ask yourself if your employees really understand why the new behavior is

---

[33]Kurt Lewin, "Frontiers in Group Dynamics: Concept, Method and Reality in Social Science; Social Equilibria and Social Change," Human Relations 1, no. 1 (1947): 7.
[34]John P. Kotter, "Leading Change: Why Transformation Efforts Fail," Harvard Business Review 73, no. 2 (1995): 59.

important. And have you explained it to them in terms that relate to their daily lives, not just in terms of KPIs?

Reflect—Honest Self-Assessment

Once people understand why change is important, the next step is to think about it. Engagement piques interest, while reflection personalizes it. This is where people honestly compare their actions to what is expected of them. This is a process of becoming more aware of yourself and seeing where you fall short.

Psychology has long demonstrated the significance of this step. Self-Regulation Theory[35] posits that individuals consistently evaluate themselves against established standards and implement modifications upon detecting discrepancies. The Johari Window[36] provides a comparable perspective: Introspection diminishes the "blind spot"—the aspects others perceive in us that we have yet to acknowledge in ourselves.

One manufacturing company had team leaders do a simple "digital skills self-audit." A lot of people were shocked to learn that they depended on junior staff for even the most basic data entry. That one exercise brought to light hidden dependencies and, even more importantly, made them more open to developing their own skills. Thinking about things made a vague sense of change into a clear understanding of what needed to be done.

The most important questions: Do I see the gaps between where I am are and where I need to be? And just as importantly, how do teams feel about their ability to move forward as a group?

Intent—The Psychological Pivot

If you reflect without a purpose, you're just stuck. People may see the gaps, but nothing will change unless they promise to do something different.

---

[35]Charles S. Carver and Michael F. Scheier, "Control Theory: A Useful Conceptual Framework for Personality–Social, Clinical, and Health Psychology," Psychological Bulletin 92, no. 1 (1982): 115.

[36]Joseph Luft and Harrington Ingham, "The Johari Window: A Graphic Model of Interpersonal Awareness," in Proceedings of the Western Training Laboratory in Group Development (University of California, Los Angeles, 1955).

Intent is the psychological pivot, the point at which motivation solidifies into behavior aimed at a goal.

Studies consistently demonstrate that this is the most significant predictor of tangible change. Ajzen's Theory of Planned Behavior[37] elucidates that intention serves as the intermediary between beliefs and actions. Self-Determination Theory[38] posits that intention is re-inforced when it is associated with autonomy, competence, and relatedness. Goal-Setting Theory[39] has shown for decades that the more specific and measurable a goal is, the more people will be committed to it.

Think about a consulting firm that started using digital time-logging. At first, workers didn't want to do it because it felt bureaucratic and intrusive. But leaders used three levers to change the focus to intent. First, freedom: "You can log in through an app, the web, or e-mail, whichever works best for you." Second, competence: Employees felt capable after learning how to speak the local languages. Third, relatedness: showing that accurate data increased team bonuses linked each person's actions to the group's results. Once intent was set, the rate of adoption went over 90 percent.

The questions for leaders are simple but important: How do we become concrete in building that intention? How are we helping workers make clear their personal commitments? And are we using autonomy, competence, and relatedness to make that intent last?

Change—Turning Intention into Habit

This is where the real test is: making your intentions turn into actions that last. Change isn't just one thing; it's doing something over and over until it becomes the norm. At this point, intention turns into a habit.

---

[37]Icek Ajzen, "The Theory of Planned Behavior," Organizational Behavior and Human Decision Processes 50, no. 2 (1991): 180.
[38]Edward L. Deci and Richard M. Ryan, Intrinsic Motivation and Self-Determination in Human Behavior (Springer, 1985).
[39]Edwin A. Locke and Gary P. Latham, A Theory of Goal Setting & Task Performance (Prentice Hall, 1990).

According to Lally et al.[40] it takes an average of 66 days for new behaviors to become stable. Skinner's classic Reinforcement Theory[41] tells us that positive reinforcement speeds up this process. The more people see small wins rewarded, the more likely they are to do the same thing again.

A telecom sales team that is using digital upselling is a good example. Instead of telling their employees to "sell more packages," managers set small goals, like making two upsell pitches every day. Along with this, they gave coaching, quick feedback, and public praise. What started as a forced effort became a habit in three months. It wasn't just a task on the list anymore; it was how they sold.

The questions for leaders are simple but very important: What ways are there to keep new behaviors going? And are people celebrating small wins often and in public enough to make change feel good?

Why ENRICH Matters

ENRICH ensures behavioral change is not accidental but structured. The pivot of Intent is particularly critical: Without it, engagement and reflection collapse into awareness without adoption. Leaders who master intent-formation will close the "knowing-doing gap" that derails many transformations. It is not about prescribing steps but, once again, about asking the important questions and keep track of the answers.

Leadership CORE5

While ENRICH focuses on the individual behavioral journey, Leadership CORE5 focuses on the leaders driving adoption. It identifies five dimensions leaders must master to create conditions for behavioral change.

Role Modeling

Hypocrisy is the quickest way to kill a change. If leaders tell people to act one way but do the opposite, people won't follow them. People don't

---

[40]Phillippa Lally, Cornelia H. M. van Jaarsveld, Henry W. W. Potts, and Jane Wardle, "How Are Habits Formed: Modelling Habit Formation in the Real World," European Journal of Social Psychology 40, no. 6 (2010): 1001.

[41]B. F. Skinner, Science and Human Behavior (Macmillan, 1953).

just hear what leaders say; they also see what leaders do. That's why role modeling is such an important part of CORE5.

Bandura's Social Learning Theory[42] raises that individuals acquire knowledge through the observation of credible models. The lesson is lost if the "model" doesn't do what they say.

Think about a big store around the world setting up a new digital HR portal. Adoption was slow until the executives did something simple: They started using the system only themselves, in front of the whole company. The effect was immediate. Staff thought, "We have to do this too if the leaders do." No orders, no memos—just a clear example.

The most important question for leaders here is simple: *Am I acting in the way I expect others to act?*

Personality

Change isn't just about systems; it's also about the people who run them. The personality traits of leaders can help or hurt adoption. Leaders who know their own strengths and weaknesses can better lead change.

For instance, research on the Big Five Personality Traits[43] shows that being open to new experiences is a good sign of being adaptable. Leader–Member Exchange (LMX) Theory[44] elucidates the influence of leader personality on trust, relationships, and, ultimately, adoption.

In one program to change things, an introverted leader thought that being quiet meant being calm. People thought they were disapproving because they didn't say anything. They learned how to frame their support clearly with coaching, which turned a problem into a strength. Once they made their approval clear, trust and acceptance grew.

The question to think about is: *How do my own traits affect how people see me when things change?*

---

[42]Albert Bandura, Social Learning Theory (Prentice Hall, 1977).

[43]Robert R. McCrae and Paul T. Costa, "A Five-Factor Theory of Personality," in Handbook of Personality: Theory and Research, 2nd ed., ed. Lawrence A. Pervin and Oliver P. John (Guilford Press, 1999).

[44]George B. Graen and Mary Uhl-Bien, "Relationship-Based Approach to Leadership: Development of Leader–Member Exchange (LMX) Theory of Leadership over 25 Years: Applying a Multi-Level Multi-Domain Perspective," The Leadership Quarterly 6, no. 2 (1995): 220.

Perception

Being technically correct isn't enough for transformation. People judge leaders not only by what they do but also by how they are seen. No matter how good your strategy is, people won't trust you if they don't see you as trustworthy.

According to research on Implicit Leadership Theories,[45] people follow people who fit their idea of what a leader should look and act like. Trust Theory[46] asserts that trust is founded on three perceptions: competence, goodwill, and honesty. Without those, perception and influence both fall apart.

A strong example came from a manager at a mid-level bank. He wasn't the most experienced or the most technical. But his workers thought he was the most trustworthy leader because he always explained his choices. What happened? His team was the first to use new digital tools, and they did so with more enthusiasm than any other group. His power came from how people saw him, not from his title.

The simple question to ask yourself is, *Do the people I lead see me as real, consistent, and trustworthy?*

Context

There is no one style of leadership that works everywhere. Leaders need to be able to change with the times in order to lead change. In times of crisis, being decisive boosts confidence; in times of growth, giving people power spurs innovation. The best leaders can change their minds without losing their focus.

This is similar to what Contingency Theories of Leadership[47] say, which is that a leader's effectiveness depends on how well their style fits the situation. It's not about being a certain type of leader; it's about knowing which type the situation calls for.

---

[45]Robert G. Lord and Karen J. Maher, Leadership and Information Processing: Linking Perceptions and Performance (Unwin Hyman, 1991).

[46]Roger C. Mayer, James H. Davis, and F. David Schoorman, "An Integrative Model of Organizational Trust," Academy of Management Review 20, no. 3 (1995): 710.

[47]Fred E. Fiedler, A Theory of Leadership Effectiveness (McGraw-Hill, 1967), 45.

Think about a logistics company. When a cyberattack brought operations to a standstill, the CEO took charge and made quick decisions, gave clear orders, and focused completely on restoring stability. When the company started an innovation program months later, the same CEO changed to participative leadership, which meant encouraging brainstorming, debate, and shared ownership. The ability to adapt became a sign of good leadership.

The most important question is: *Am I changing my style to fit the situation of the change, or am I stuck in one way of doing things?*

Individuality

Change doesn't need leaders who are the same. It wants real ones. Employees can easily spot "textbook behaviors" that have been practiced. What inspires is individuality—leaders bringing their own voice, style, and humanity into the process.

Authentic Leadership Theory[48] says that leaders who are self-aware and open about their relationships are more trusted. Being real, not perfect, is what authenticity is all about.

This was perfectly shown by the founder of a South American start-up. Instead of using a stiff "corporate tone" in transformation workshops, she used her natural humor and storytelling. The sessions were memorable, interesting, and inspiring because she was herself, not because she followed a script.

The question to think about is: *Am I using my unique qualities to inspire others, or am I hiding behind templates?*

A Behavioral Symphony

When combined, these three models form a powerful behavioral engine:

- McKinsey's Influence Model provides the structural levers (understanding, mechanisms, skills, role modeling).

---

[48]Bruce J. Avolio and William L. Gardner, "Authentic Leadership Development: Getting to the Root of Positive Forms of Leadership," The Leadership Quarterly 16, no. 3 (2005): 317.

- ENRICH provides the inner journey of behavioral adoption (engage, reflect, intent, change).
- CORE5 ensures leaders themselves are equipped to influence authentically across contexts.

Practical Case: Digital Twin in Real Estate

A consultancy launched a digital twin business for property searches. Adoption lagged among staff. They applied the models:

- Influence Model: communicated "why" (faster client searches), set KPIs, trained staff, and had leaders use the system
- ENRICH: Staff reflected on their digital literacy, set personal intentions to process 80 percent of searches digitally, and reinforced behaviors with feedback
- CORE5: Leaders role-modeled adoption, adjusted their style, and reinforced perceptions of authenticity

Result: within 12 months, the digital twin business overtook the parent's traditional segment.

Behavioral Adoption as the Heart of Transformation

No matter how robust the strategy, how innovative the technology, or how detailed the process, transformation fails without behavioral adoption. The Influence Model, ENRICH, and CORE5 together form a behavioral playbook for transformation:

- Influence Model: the structural architecture
- ENRICH: the psychological pathway
- CORE5: the leadership enabler

For me, these models are not just frameworks. They are anchors for transformation programs, and leadership journeys. They remind us that transformation is ultimately not about systems—it is about people. And people change not when told to, but when engaged, inspired, and led.

CHAPTER 10

Talent, Leadership, and Culture

In many companies, people are the only element that truly makes them competitive. You can copy technology, copy processes, and figure out how to make products work. But it's not only hard to find people with the same skills, knowledge, and experience; it's also often impossible to find someone else who can do the same job without losing a lot of value. But in digital transformation programs, businesses often spend too much on technology and not enough on people. Money is spent on systems, but the people who will use them and decide if they work are not ready. The result is advanced technology that doesn't work very well.

People have had to deal with a constant stream of changes over the past 15 years: the global financial crisis, waves of technological disruption, the COVID-19 pandemic, and now the speed-up of AI. The strength shown has been amazing. But the failure rates of transformation programs are still very high It's not always "bad technology" that causes the problem. It is almost always about people— their preparation, support, and involvement in the journey.

Professor Clayton Christensen said that to make a change, you need to work on resources, processes, and the profit formula all at once. Organizations often change processes or look for new ways to make money without paying attention to their resources, especially their people. Organizations don't just do true transformation; they live it.

This chapter makes the case that talent is what makes change possible. Bad talent will break the best model, but good talent can make even bad models work. Companies that put people at the center of their digital transformation efforts are more likely to succeed.

Here my top five areas to focus when it comes down to people.

Beyond One Workforce

There is never a single type of worker. There are digital natives, digital migrants, skeptics, pioneers, introverts, extroverts, resisters, and champions on teams. Treating all of your employees the same way is a sure way to fail.

From the standpoint of organizational psychology, motivation is not homogeneous.[49] reminds us that people have different needs, such as safety, belonging, esteem, and self-actualization. Herzberg et al.'s[50] two-factor theory shows how motivators (growth, recognition) are different from hygiene factors (salary, working conditions).

Practical Cases

- Telecom rollout: A European telecom company rolled out a new digital CRM, and younger employees quickly got used to it, but mid-career staff didn't want to. Leaders figured out that it wasn't laziness; it was fear of not being good enough. A peer-to-peer coaching program that paired digital natives with immigrants tripled the number of people who used it in six months.
- SME manufacturing company: Engineers at an SME didn't like digital dashboards until managers changed their minds and said they were "tools to free your time for innovation." Adoption changed when workers knew "what's in it for me."

Key question

Have we not only mapped roles but also groups based on their motivation and readiness?

---

[49]Abraham H. Maslow, "A Theory of Human Motivation," Psychological Review 50, no. 4 (1943): 372.
[50]Frederick Herzberg, Bernard Mausner, and Barbara B. Snyderman, The Motivation to Work, 2nd ed. (John Wiley & Sons, 1959).

Processes Create Clarity, Bureaucracy Kills Energy

For clarity, consistency, and growth, processes are very important. Bureaucracy, on the other hand, is a process that doesn't have a goal. It takes away energy, lowers motivation, and makes people less interested.

The Job Demands–Resources (JD-R) model[51] illustrates that an increase in demands (such as paperwork and unnecessary approvals) without a corresponding increase in resources (such as autonomy, clarity, and tools) elevates the risk of burnout.

Practical Cases

- Insurance company: It took weeks to process claims because there were six levels of approval. Reducing the number of approvals to two cut the time it took to get things done by 70 percent and made employees happier. Processes made things clear, while bureaucracy slowed things down.
- Logistics SME: By automating the creation of invoices, staff members saved 30 percent of their time on administrative tasks. "I don't feel like a robot anymore," one worker said. A small change to the process got rid of bureaucratic weight, which made people feel better and added value.

Key question

Are our processes making things clear or hidden bureaucracy is wasting energy?

The Power of Involvement

Most of the time, top-down orders don't create ownership. It's common but wrong to announce a change by e-mail and expect people to follow it. Adoption is driven by involvement instead.

---

[51]Arnold B. Bakker and Evangelia Demerouti, "The Job Demands-Resources Model: State of the Art," Journal of Managerial Psychology 22, no. 3 (2007): 312.

McGregor's[52] Theory X and Theory Y exemplifies this: Leaders who perceive employees as resistant (Theory X) enforce change; conversely, those who regard them as self-motivated (Theory Y) encourage participation.

Practical Cases

- Redesigning banking: A European bank changed the way it signed up new customers. Instead of HQ writing scripts, teams at the branch level worked together to make workflows. Compared to a competitor's top-down rollout, which staff didn't like, adoption went through the roof.
- A tech start-up invited frontline engineers to sprint demos, but a legacy company did not. In the new company, adoption went smoothly, but in the old company, engineers messed up the rollout by "forgetting" to use the system.

Key question

How are employees cocreating change, rather than passively receiving it?

Giving Teams a Voice

Listening doesn't mean doing everything your employees ask you to do. It is about making them feel like they are being heard, which makes them less likely to fight back and makes them feel safer psychologically.

Amy Edmondson's[53] research on psychological safety demonstrates that teams in which individuals feel secure to express their opinions excel in innovation and adaptability.

---

[52]Douglas McGregor, The Human Side of Enterprise (McGraw-Hill, 1960).
[53]Amy C. Edmondson, "Psychological Safety and Learning Behavior in Work Teams," Administrative Science Quarterly 44, no. 2 (1999): 352.

Practical Cases

- A fashion brand called "ideathon" had thousands of employees come up with ideas during the digital acceleration phase. Some ideas were not put into action, but listening made people feel like they owned them. Staff said, "It feels like we had a hand in the change."
- Change in retail: A retailer that was being hurt by e-commerce started town halls where employees could ask the CEO anything. Employees who were doubtful said, "At least they listen now." Resistance went down, and engagement went up.

Key question

Do our people feel safe to voice concerns without fear of being ignored or punished?

The Turning Point of Change

This is the anchor strategy. At best, instruction ("do this") gets people to follow the rules. Intention, expressed as "I want to do this," engenders transformation.

Ajzen's[54] Theory of Planned Behavior demonstrates that intention is a more accurate predictor of action than awareness. Deci and Ryan's[55] Self-Determination Theory elucidates that intrinsic motivation arises from autonomy, competence, and relatedness.

Why intention is important

- Awareness without intention is like thinking about something without doing anything about it.
- Intention is the choice you make to change.
- Leaders create intention by making change personally significant.

---

[54]Ajzen, "The Theory of Planned Behavior," 180.
[55]Deci and Ryan, Intrinsic Motivation.

Practical Cases

- A big logistics company's cybersecurity crisis: After a €400 million cyberattack, new rules were framed as heroic ("You are protecting global trade"). Not only did employees follow the rules, but they were proud of it. Adoption sped up.
- Mrs. Sarah's shop: At first, the staff didn't want to go digital when Sara did. Her staff only accepted the new tools when Sara changed the way she talked about them to "keeping our shop alive for the next generation." Not instruction but intention made people commit.

Key question

How are we moving people from "I know I need to change" to "I choose to change"?

PART 5

Sustaining to Evolve

Because Transformation Is Never Finished

Delivery changes the results, and people keep the change going. We talk about the human and leadership work that makes new ways of doing things stick, and then we go back to being ready to explain why some changes work and others don't.

At some point during every change, people must stop doing things and start thinking. At that point, the question changes from "What have we built?" to "What will last?" To change while staying the same, organizations need to make sure that progress is in their DNA. It's about turning short-term wins into long-term skills. Companies that do well don't just change once; they learn how to change all the time.

This is the last part of our journey. We learn that leaders who stay the same even when things are unclear, cultures that encourage curiosity and responsibility, and systems that change without losing their coherence are the keys to long-term success. We talk about how people become stewards of change instead of subjects of it, how readiness grows over time, and how every ending should lead to a new beginning.

At its core, change isn't a project. It's a way of thinking, and to keep it going, you need to grow with purpose, clarity, and conviction.

CHAPTER 11

A Company's Readiness Through FRAME

In the first few chapters of this book, we discussed the five pillars of success and readiness in digital transformation, represented in the FRAME model. FRAME is not just a way of structuring ideas.

It is the lens through which we can understand both why some companies succeed in digital transformation while others fail.

- Formula (Business Model)
- Relevance (Market)
- Alignment (Strategy)
- Muscle (Organization)
- Engine (Processes)

Each of these pillars defines much of what a company is, but they also determine how well a transformation will be executed. When companies succeed, it is usually because their FRAME is solid. When they fail, it is because one or more of these elements are weak, ignored, or misaligned.

It is never easy to pinpoint success or failure down to a single factor. Transformation is complex, systemic, and shaped by context. Still, across my years of leading transformations and discussing experiences with leaders across Europe, I have seen recurring patterns. These lessons are especially critical for SMEs, which often have fewer resources to absorb mistakes.

This chapter explores each pillar of FRAME, showing what strengthens it, what weakens it, and how leaders can use these insights to navigate their transformation journey.

Reinventing How You Create Value

Business models and its formula are the blueprint of value creation. If the blueprint is outdated, no amount of tactical optimization will save the company.

Some patterns I see happening regularly:

1. **New business models set up "on the side"**
   As we explored in the Silent disruption and digital twins subchapter, legacy structures resist radical change. Creating new models in parallel—outside the old walls—often gives them a fighting chance.

2. **Digital twins as proactive disruption**
   Rather than waiting to be disrupted, companies can create their own disruptive "twin." Booking.com, for instance, was essentially a digital twin of the travel agency, designed for a lower rung of the ladder.

3. **Start small, test, and grow**
   Discipline matters here. Testing hypotheses (see previous chapter) on a small scale allows for correction before large investments. Fail fast, learn, iterate.

4. **Excellence in standardized areas**
   Not everything needs reinvention. Areas that are commoditized must at least meet the industry benchmark. Falling behind here destroys credibility.

When Formula is weak, companies cling to models that no longer scale, and miss the chance to reinvent themselves before disruption hits.

Competing in the Right Arena

A brilliant strategy means nothing if you are aiming at the wrong market, or if you misunderstand your positioning. Being relevant to the right customer at the right marketplace.

Some patterns I see happening regularly:

1. **Clear market positioning**
   Companies must know not only whom they compete against but also what their unique differentiator is. "Who is our customer?

Why do they choose us?" If the answer is vague, the market will be brutal.

2. **Recent and reliable market analysis**
SMEs often fly blind here. But without updated data, decisions are based on assumptions that may no longer be true. Transformation decisions must sit on current market insight.

3. **Continuous analysis—especially of start-ups**
Silent disruption often comes from small players. Leaders must systematically scan for these signals. Arrogance ("those start-ups can't compete with us") is one of the fastest routes to being blindsided.

4. **Protecting and investing in competitive advantages**
Transformation should sharpen your edges, not blunt them. Knowing where you truly win—and doubling down on that—is critical.

When Relevant is weak, companies optimize for a market that no longer exists and wake up too late when customers shift elsewhere.

The Anchor of Direction

Without strategy, execution is chaos. But with poorly articulated strategy, execution is just as doomed. The clear alignment goes a long way.

Some patterns I see happening regularly:

1. **Ability to articulate strategy at all levels**
A strategy that only lives in PowerPoint is not a strategy. It must be communicated and understood across the organization. Leaders at all levels need to articulate it clearly so that every team member sees where they fit. Without this alignment, people work hard but pull in different directions.

2. **Ability to think long-term despite short-term fires**
SMEs, in particular (though applicable to any company), are pressured daily by operational challenges. It takes discipline and talent to keep sight of a multiyear vision. The best companies cultivate leaders who balance both lenses: fix the short term while never losing sight of the horizon.

3. **Focus on strategic over tactical**

The Four-Floor Model, discussed earlier, provides a discipline: linking activities directly to key results and vision. Tactical actions matter, but if they are not aligned to the strategic initiative, they consume energy without building the future.

When Alignment is weak, companies waste resources, get trapped in tactical firefighting, and stall their transformation.

The Human Core of Transformation

Technology may be the tool, but people and its organization are the muscle.

Some patterns I see happening regularly:

1. **Leadership with digital embedded**

Transformation cannot be delegated. Leaders must embody digital thinking themselves. A "do as I say, not as I do" culture kills credibility.

2. **Commercial strategy linked to digital**

Digital commerce is not a side experiment—it must be embedded in the overall commercial strategy.

3. **Sales force as ambassadors**

Sales teams are the frontline. If they don't understand and believe in the transformation, the market won't either.

4. **Incentives aligned with digital goals**

Misaligned incentives are silent killers. If incentives reward the old behaviors, people will continue them—regardless of the vision.

5. **Invest in digital literacy**

As discussed in the People chapter, digital literacy is no longer optional. Employees who lack it cannot fully contribute. The quadrant approach helps prioritize where to focus.

When Muscle is weak, transformation plans collapse under cultural resistance, misaligned incentives, and lack of skills.

Turning Vision into Motion

Processes are the operational heartbeat. If the heartbeat falters, even the best vision dies.

Some patterns I see happening regularly:

1. **Map processes with customer journeys**
   Success lies in integration: aligning internal processes with the external customer experience.
2. **Clarity on top processes**
   Every company should know the 5 to 10 processes that determine success. If leaders cannot name them, the organization is flying blind.
3. **Map journeys, value chains, and overlaps**
   True efficiency comes from mapping where customer journeys and value chains intersect—the pressure points where experiences are made or broken.
4. **Remove exceptions instead of adding them**
   Companies scale through standardization. Exceptions create cost, confusion, and complexity. Discipline in removing them is key.

When Engine is weak, inefficiency erodes margins, frustrates customers, and prevents scaling.

Why FRAME Predicts Success or Failure

FRAME is not a checklist. It is a system. Each pillar reinforces the others.

- If Alignment is unclear, even the strongest Muscle cannot pull in the right direction.
- If the Formula is outdated, investments in the Engine will only optimize the wrong model.
- If the Market is misunderstood, all other pillars will eventually collapse.

This is why I insist that transformation is not about "implementing digital." It is about Thinking Digital—embedding these pillars into the DNA of how the company sees itself, competes, and organizes its future.

It is like learning a foreign language. At first, you translate word by word, painfully. That is "implementing digital." Over time, you stop translating and start thinking in the language. That is "Thinking Digital." FRAME is the grammar of that language.

Companies that master it succeed. Those that don't fail.

CHAPTER 12

Beyond Digital, Toward What's Next

Writing this book has been both a personal ambition and a professional necessity. For years I have carried the desire to organize my experiences, frameworks, and reflections on digital transformation into something coherent and accessible—not because I believe I have all the answers but because I know how disorienting and overwhelming this journey can be. If the pages you've just read provide even a few moments of clarity, a model that simplifies a complex reality, or a story that sparks an idea, then this effort has been worth it.

The phrase "Think Digital, Beyond Digital" has guided me throughout this process. It is not a slogan, nor is it a piece of motivational rhetoric. It is a mindset. It means acknowledging the undeniable complexity of digital transformation while also refusing to be paralyzed by it. Complexity cannot be eliminated, but it can be structured, simplified, and made actionable. That is why I built models like the FRAME pillars, the Four-Floor Model, ENRICH, ASCEND, Leadership CORE5, or SCRIPT. These are not academic abstractions; they are tools born of real-world practice, forged in conversations with leaders, in trial-and-error projects, and in the lived reality of organizations under pressure to transform. They don't provide you the answer; rather, they help to question enough to get to the answers.

Still, no model guarantees certainty. There will be moments of doubt. There will be external shocks—pandemics, crises, disruptions—that remind us how little control we truly have. But doubt is not failure. Doubt is evidence that we are grappling with real problems, and it should not deter us from continuing the journey. Transformation is not about avoiding turbulence; it is about building resilience to keep moving despite it.

One thing I have learned without question is that the market does not wait. It does not pause for companies to debate "if" digital transformation should happen, nor does it indulge the illusion of "when" being some far-off horizon. The only relevant question is "how," and the only valid answer to "when" is "now." Those who delay discover too late that they are already behind.

At the same time, execution is not just about technology. It is about people. People are not abstract "resources." They are human beings with energy, fears, talents, and limits. If leaders find digital transformation difficult, then imagine how much more challenging it is for employees who do not get to make the big decisions yet must live with their consequences. They also get tired. They also question whether this is worth it. They also have bad days. For this reason, I insist that the people factor is the centerpiece of every transformation (buyers, employees, suppliers— all are built with people). Processes can be redesigned, strategies rewritten, and technologies replaced. But without people who believe, adapt, and grow, no transformation lasts.

I urge every leader reading this to treat humility as a strategic advantage. None of us has all the answers. The problems we face today have likely been faced by others before us. Reach out. Use LinkedIn to connect. Share experiences over a coffee chat. Learn from those who have failed and those who have succeeded. In writing this book, I spoke with many leaders, read extensively, and reflected deeply—not because I lacked confidence but because I know knowledge grows in networks, not in isolation. Humility is not weakness; it is wisdom.

My hope is that these pages serve as both a practical guide and a source of encouragement. We have explored customers and markets, business models and strategies, execution and adoption, culture and leadership. We have moved from analysis to planning, from vision to action. It is a lot of information, and it should not be rushed. Like learning a new language, transformation only becomes fluent with practice, repetition, and application. At first, it feels clumsy, as if everything must be translated. But over time, the concepts and tools become natural. They stop being "digital initiatives" and simply become "how the company works."

This is especially important for SMEs. SMEs have less room for mistakes, fewer resources to waste, and often have to deal with life-or-death situations when they start to change These companies also have something that bigger companies want: the ability to change quickly. These companies can skip steps, adopt models more quickly, and create value in ways that big companies can't if they stay focused and disciplined. Many of the frameworks I've shared are made with this in mind: to give any company structure without making it feel overwhelmed, clarity without creating the impression of bureaucracy, and tools that grow with its goals.

In the end, this book is my way of helping to make digital transformation knowledge available to everyone. I want to make sure that every leader and every business, big or small, has access to models that can help them do well. Success in digital transformation means more than just staying alive in the digital economy. It's about letting people be creative, strong, and reach their full potential.

And as you go on, I leave you with one last thought: Change should also be fun. We take away its meaning if we only talk about stress, KPIs, and deadlines. Success isn't just about the end result; it's also about the journey. It's about the creativity it sparks, the teamwork it encourages, and, yes, even the fun it brings. This all makes a lot less sense without fun and happiness.

I wish you success in your transformations—but more than that, I wish you journeys that are transformative, creative, resilient, and full of moments of laughter and discovery. That, more than anything, is the true meaning of *thinking digital, beyond digital.*

Bibliography

Adidas Group. "Annual Report 2024." Digital Report, 2025. Accessed August 31, 2025. https://report.adidas-group.com/2024/en/.

Ajzen, Icek. "The Theory of Planned Behavior." *Organizational Behavior and Human Decision Processes* 50, no. 2 (1991): 179–211.

Bakker, Arnold B., and Evangelia Demerouti. "The Job Demands–Resources Model: State of the Art." *Journal of Managerial Psychology* 22, no. 3 (2007): 309–28.

Bandura, Albert. *Social Learning Theory*. Prentice Hall, 1977.

Basford, Tessa, and Bill Schaninger. "The Four Building Blocks of Change." *McKinsey Quarterly*, April 11, 2016. Accessed September 2, 2025. https://www.mckinsey.com/capabilities/people-and-organizational-performance/our-insights/the-four-building-blocks--of-change.

CaixaBank Research. "E-Commerce in Portugal during the Pandemic: A Buffer for the Fall in Consumption?" October 18, 2021. Accessed August 31, 2025. https://www.caixabankresearch.com/en/economics-markets/recent-developments/e-commerce-portugal-during-pandemic-buffer-fall-consumption.

Carver, Charles S., and Michael F. Scheier. "Control Theory: A Useful Conceptual Framework for Personality–Social, Clinical, and Health Psychology." *Psychological Bulletin* 92, no. 1 (1982): 111–35.

Christensen, Clayton M. *The Innovator's Dilemma: When New Technologies Cause Great Firms to Fail*. Harvard Business School Press, 1997.

Christensen, Clayton M., Taddy Hall, Karen Dillon, and David S. Duncan. "Know Your Customers' 'Jobs to Be Done.'" *Harvard Business Review*, September 2016. https://www.hbs.edu/faculty/Pages/item.aspx?num=51553.

Deci, Edward L., and Richard M. Ryan. *Intrinsic Motivation and Self-Determination in Human Behavior*. Springer, 1985.

Drucker Institute. "About Peter Drucker." Accessed August 31, 2025. https://drucker.institute/about-peter-drucker.

Ecommerce Europe and EuroCommerce. "2021 *European E-commerce Report (Light Version)."* September 23, 2021. Accessed August 31, 2025. https://ecommerce-europe.eu/publication/2021-european-e-commerce-report-light-version/.

Edmondson, Amy C. "Psychological Safety and Learning Behavior in Work Teams." *Administrative Science Quarterly* 44, no. 2 (1999): 350–83.

Fiedler, Fred E. *A Theory of Leadership Effectiveness*. McGraw-Hill, 1967.

Fitriasari, Fika. "How Do Small and Medium Enterprises (SMEs) Survive the COVID-19 Outbreak?" *Jurnal Inovasi Ekonomi* 5, no. 2 (2020): 53–62.

Graen, George B., and Mary Uhl-Bien. "Relationship-Based Approach to Lead-ership: Development of Leader–Member Exchange (LMX) Theory of Leadership Over 25 Years: Applying a Multi-Level Multi-Domain Perspective." *The Leadership Quarterly* 6, no. 2 (1995): 219–47.

Grieves, Michael, and John Vickers. "Digital Twin: Mitigating Unpredictable, Undesirable Emergent Behavior in Complex Systems." In *Trans-Disciplinary Perspectives on System Complexity*, edited by F.-J. Kahlen, S. Flumerfelt, and A. Alves. Springer, 2017.

Hervé, Annaële, Christophe Schmitt, and Rico Baldegger. "Digitalization, Entrepre-neurial Orientation and Internationalization of Micro-, Small-, and Medium-Sized Enterprises." *Technology Innovation Management Review* 10, no. 4 (2020): 5–17.

Herzberg, Frederick, Bernard Mausner, and Barbara B. Snyderman. *The Motiva-tion to Work*. 2nd ed. John Wiley & Sons, 1959.

Investor's Business Daily. "Amazon Takes Walmart's Revenue Crown (For Now)." February 20, 2025. https://www.investors.com/news/technology/amazon-stock-walmart-revenue-amzn-wmt/. Accessed August 31, 2025.

Jenkinson, Angus. "Beyond Segmentation." *Journal of Targeting, Measurement and Analysis for Marketing* 3, no. 1 (1994): 60–72.

Kotter, John P. "Leading Change: Why Transformation Efforts Fail." *Harvard Business Review* 73, no. 2 (1995): 59–67.

Lally, Phillippa, Cornelia H. M. van Jaarsveld, Henry W. W. Potts, and Jane Wardle. "How Are Habits Formed: Modelling Habit Formation in the Real World." *European Journal of Social Psychology* 40, no. 6 (2010): 998–1009.

Lee, Yan-Yin, Mohammad Falahat, and Bik-Kai Sia. "Impact of Digitalization on the Speed of Internationalization." *International Business Research* 12, no. 4 (2019): 1–11.

Lewin, Kurt. "Frontiers in Group Dynamics: Concept, Method and Reality in Social Science; Social Equilibria and Social Change." *Human Relations* 1, no. 1 (1947): 5–41.

Libert, Barry, Megan Beck, and Yoram Wind. "7 Questions to Ask before Your Next Digital Transformation." *Harvard Business Review*, March 2016. https://hbr.org/2016/07/7-questions-to-ask-before-your-next-digital-transformation.

Locke, Edwin A., and Gary P. Latham. *A Theory of Goal Setting & Task Perfor-mance*. Prentice Hall, 1990.

Lord, Robert G., and Karen J. Maher. *Leadership and Information Processing: Linking Perceptions and Performance*. Unwin Hyman, 1991.

Luft, Joseph, and Harrington Ingham. "The Johari Window: A Graphic Model of Interpersonal Awareness." In *Proceedings of the Western Training Laboratory in Group Development*. University of California, Los Angeles, 1955.

Martin, Roger L. "Strategy Isn't What You Say, It's What You Do." *Harvard Business Review*, June 18, 2014. https://hbr.org/2014/06/strategy-isnt-what-you-say-its-what-you-do.

Maslow, Abraham H. "A Theory of Human Motivation." *Psychological Review* 50, no. 4 (1943): 370–96.

Mayer, Roger C., James H. Davis, and F. David Schoorman. "An Integrative Model of Organizational Trust." *Academy of Management Review* 20, no. 3 (1995): 709–34.

McCrae, Robert R., and Paul T. Costa. "A Five-Factor Theory of Personality." In *Handbook of Personality: Theory and Research*, 2nd ed., edited by Lawrence A. Pervin and Oliver P. John. Guilford Press, 1999.

McGregor, Douglas. *The Human Side of Enterprise.* McGraw-Hill, 1960.

Menold, Jessica, Kathryn W. Jablokow, Timothy W. Simpson, and Emily A. Waterman. "The Prototype for X (PFX) Framework: Assessing Its Impact on Students' Prototyping Awareness." Paper presented at the ASEE Annual Conference & Exposition, New Orleans, June 26–29, 2016.

Osterwalder, Alexander, and Yves Pigneur. *Business Model Generation: A Handbook for Visionaries, Game Changers, and Challengers.* John Wiley & Sons, 2010.

Porter, Michael E. *Competitive Advantage: Creating and Sustaining Superior Performance.* Free Press, 1985.

Pruitt, John S., and Jonathan Grudin. "Personas: Practice and Theory." In *Proceedings of the 2003 Conference on Designing for User Experiences (DUX '03).* Association for Computing Machinery, 2003. https://doi.org/10.1145/997078.997089.

Sahut, Jean-Michel, Luca Iandoli, and Frédéric Teulon. "The Age of Digital Entrepreneurship." *Small Business Economics* 56, no. 3 (2021): 1159–69. https://doi.org/10.1007/s11187-019-00260-8.

Silva, Rui Pedro, Henrique São Mamede, and Vitor Santos. "Clarification of the Present Understanding of the Assessment of an Organization's Digital Readiness in SMEs." *Emerging Science Journal* 7, no. 6 (2023): 2279–307.

Silva, Rui Pedro, Henrique São Mamede, and Vitor Santos. "A New Proposed Model to Assess the Digital Organizational Readiness to Maximize the Results of the Digital Transformation in SMEs." *Journal of Innovation & Knowledge* 10, no. 1 (2025): 100644.

Skinner, B. F. *Science and Human Behavior.* Macmillan, 1953.

Smith, Wendell R. "Product Differentiation and Market Segmentation as Alternative Marketing Strategies." *Journal of Marketing* 21, no. 1 (1956): 3–8.

Temkin, Bruce D. *Mapping the Customer Journey.* Forrester Research report, February 5, 2010. https://crowdsynergy.wdfiles.com/local--files/customer-journey-mapping/mapping_customer_journey.pdf.

Tynan, Caroline A., and Jennifer Drayton. "Market Segmentation," *Journal of Marketing Management* 2, no. 3 (1987): 301–35. https://doi.org/10.1080/0267257X.1987.9964020.

About the Author

 **Rui Pedro Silva** is a global executive leader, researcher, and speaker whose work sits at the intersection of digital transformation, leadership, and organizational psychology. With more than 20 years of international experience across industries, Rui has led transformation and leadership development at some of the world's most recognized companies, including Puma, Adidas and A.P. Moller-Maersk, where he served in senior executive roles.

He holds a PhD in organizational readiness for digital transformation and a master's in organizational psychology, combining scientific rigor with real-world leadership practice. Rui is the author of several peer-reviewed publications on digital transformation, including in top ranked scientific journals such as *Journal of Innovation & Knowledge* (Elsevier, 2025).

As the founder of ThinkingLead, Rui developed a portfolio of proprietary frameworks—ASCEND, FRAME, SCRIPT, ENRICH, ALIGN, and CORE5—that guide organizations and leaders through readiness, culture, strategy, and behavioral change.

Rui is also a TEDx speaker, faculty professor, and hosted of two successful podcasts—*Talk It Thru*, featuring ordinary people creating extraordinary impact, and *Let's Talk Football (Portuguese)*, exploring leadership lessons from sport.

Through his work, Rui invites leaders to pause, reflect, and think transformation through, following ThinkingLead motto, "we don't tell you what to do; we help you think it through."

Index

Acceptance, 1–2, 3, 9, 11, 13
Adaptation, 15
Adidas, 156
AI-assisted claim triage, 198
Airbnb, 16, 72, 85, 119
Ajzen's Theory of Planned Behavior,
    201, 211
Alibaba, 156
Amazon, 3, 16, 67, 76, 104, 111,
    119, 155, 156, 159, 160, 162
A.P. Moller-Maersk, 123
Apple, 67, 94
Artificial intelligence (AI), 144–145,
    167, 207
ASCEND approach, 1–8, 11
ASCEND Modeling Canvas,
    183–185
Authentic Leadership Theory, 205

B2B, 62, 69, 156, 159
B2C, 69, 156, 159
Bad technology, 207
Bandura's Social Learning Theory, 203
Bankruptcies, 11
Behavioral change
    behavioral symphony, 205–206
        digital twin in real estate, 206
    ENRICH framework, 199–202
        change, 201–202
        engage, 199–200
        intent, 200–201
        reflect, 200
    Leadership CORE5, 202–205
        context, 204–205
        individuality, 205
        perception, 204
        personality, 203
        role modeling, 202–203
    McKinsey's Influence Model, 198
        insurance call centers, 198
Blockchain, 167
Booking system, 194
Booking.com, 154

Business Model Canvas (BMC),
    178–180, 182, 185, 187
Business model revolution, 103
Business strategy, 116–122
Bynco, 14, 119

Caixa Bank, 155, 159
Campaigns, 54
Capital and capabilities, SCRIPT
    framework, 190–191
Change management, 7, 115
Christensen, Clayton, 71, 79,
    145–148, 146, 207
Cloud computing, 142, 167
Coca-Cola, 161
Company's positioning, 39–41
Contingency Theories of
    Leadership, 204
COVID-19 pandemic, 12, 63, 155,
    159, 170, 180, 207
Customer
    definition of, 63–65
    Jobs to Be Done, 71–74
    journey and value chain, 85–100
        Natural Cleaning, 99–100
    and market, 1–2, 4–5
    personas, 68–71
    problem, and value, 74–85
        Materials Company, 81–82
    segmentation, 65–68
Customer centricity, 62
Customer journey, 85–100
Customer Relationship Management
    (CRM) system, 32
Customers, digital self-service for, 190

Dalí, Salvador, 158
Darwin, Charles, 15
Deci and Ryan's Self-Determination
    Theory, 211
Decision making, 178–185
Deliveroo, 147
Digital adds, 62

Digital commerce, 155–162
Digital loyalty, 193
Digital point-of-sale system, European
        store, 199
Digital Services Economy, 141–145
Digital transformation, 110, 127,
        173–174
    10 strategic levers, 104–106
    adaptation, 15
    Bynco, 14
    competition, 17
    definition of, 15
    digitalization, 13–14, 16
    external positioning, 55–56
    foundation, 60
    four blocks of, 43–50
    JTBD, 73
    Mr. Francis restaurant, 17–18
    organization, 30–32
    Our Clothes, 11–12, 15
    personas, 70
    principle, 16
    process risks, 57–60
    processes, 32–33
    reflection, 12–13
    starting point, 21
    technology, 51–53
    timing, 16
    value, 84
Digital twins, 145–151
Digital upselling, telecom sales
        team, 202
Digitalization, 13–14, 16
    two faces of, 18–19
Drive people and change, 1–2, 6–7
Drucker, Peter, 58
Dual-level governance model, 194

E-commerce, 155–162, 191
eBay, 160
EBITDA (earnings before interest,
        taxes, depreciation, and
        amortization), 127
Edmondson, Amy, 210
Elevator pitch, 109, 111, 115
Engineers, SME, 208
ENRICH framework, 199–202
ERP (enterprise resource planning)
        system, 13, 21

Etsy, 160
European telecom company, 208
External positioning, 55–56

Facebook, 80–81
Fashion brand, 54
Flexport, 42
Four-Floor Model, 5, 105, 113,
        123–140, 171, 182, 185,
        187, 218, 221
    analyzing investments, 138–140
    broad and granular applications, 124
    The First Floor, 125–126
    The Fourth Floor, 130–133
    limitations and ideal cases,
        136–137
    The Second Floor, 127–128
    and strategy, 137–138
    The Third Floor, 128–130
    two key applications, 125
    vision, 123–124
FRAME model, 26–33, 44–45
    alignment, 26, 29–30
    anchor of direction, 217–218
    engine, 26, 32–33
    formula, 26–28
    human core of transformation, 218
    muscle, 26, 30–32
    pillars of, 178, 215, 221
    predicts success or failure, 219–220
    reinventing how you create value, 216
    relevance, 26, 28–29
    right arena, competing in, 216–217
    turning vision into motion, 219
Fulfillment by Amazon (FBA), 144, 155

Generative AI, 105, 141, 144,
        162–167, 169, 182
Globalization, 151–154
Glovo, 51
Goal-Setting Theory, 201
Google, 126, 162

Half-marathon analogy, 57
Hervé, Annaële, 151
HR-as-a- Service, 142
Humility, 222
Hypocrisy, change, 202–203
Hypothesis-driven strategy, 170–178

IBM, 115
Ideathon, 211
IKEA, 114, 126
Implementation, SCRIPT framework,
    192–193
Implicit Leadership Theories, 204
Infrastructure-as-a-Service (IaaS), 142
Instagram, 158, 160–162
Investment analysis, 138–140
iPhone, 13, 94

Jenkinson, Angus, 68
Job Demands–Resources (JD-R)
    model, 209
Jobs, Steve, 79
Jobs to Be Done (JTBD) theory,
    71–74, 146
The Johari Window, 200

Kotter, John, 199
Kurt Lewin's Change Theory, 199

Ladder of sophistication, 146–149
Leader–Member Exchange (LMX)
    Theory, 203
Leadership, 7, 49, 78, 134, 164, 166,
    192, 198, 204–212
Leadership CORE5, 202–205
Leading change, 199
Lee, Yan-Yin, 151
Logistics-as-a-Service (LaaS), 103, 142
Logistics company, 55
Logistics Services, 41–43
L'Oréal, 161

Maersk Group, 152
Market, high-level view of, 33
    Logistics Services, 41–43
    Mrs. Joanne and Mr. Edward shoe
        shop, 34–35
    Repair Services, 35–39
Martin, Roger, 121
McGregor's Theory X and
    Theory Y, 210
McKinsey's Influence Model, 198
Menold, Jessica, 171
Mercado Libre, 160
Microsoft, 126
Mirror blindness, 4

Narrative, 55, 112, 116, 117
Netflix, 28, 67, 76, 104, 158, 167
New behavior, 199–200
Nike, 161

Organization, 30–32
Our Clothes, 11–12, 15

Payments-as-a-Service, 142
Personality, change, 203
Personas, customer, 68–71
Platform-as-a-Service (PaaS),
    142, 168
Point of Success, 74–85
Porter, Michael, 86–88
Power of involvement, 209–210
PRFAQ (Press Release, Frequently
    Asked Questions), 111–112
Problem, customer, 74–85
Product Differentiation and Market
    Segmentation as Alternative
    Marketing Strategies, 66
Progress, SCRIPT framework, 193
Psychological safety, 210

Repair Services, 35–39
Resistance, challenge of, 102–103
Risk management, 57–60
Roadmap, SCRIPT framework,
    191–192

SCRIPT framework
    capital and capabilities, 190–191
        retail company, 191
    with governance, 194–195
    implementation, 192–193
        furniture manufacturer, 192
    progress, 193
        retail group, 193
    roadmap, 191–192
        health care provider, 191–192
    scope, 189–190
        insurance company, 190
    tracking, 194
        logistics company, 194
Segmentation, customer, 65–68
Self-Determination Theory, 201
Self-reflection, 1–2, 4, 22
Self-Regulation Theory, 200

Short-term thinking, 58
Silent disruption, 145–151
Skinner's classic Reinforcement
        Theory, 202
Skou, Soren, 123
Skyscanner, 154
Smith, Wendell R., 66
Social commerce, 160, 162
Software-as-a-Service (SaaS), 142, 168
Start-ups, 12, 29, 82, 102
Strategy, 1–2, 5–6, 26, 29–30, 190
    common pitfalls, 118
    digital transformation, 117
    Four-Floor Model 137–138
    FRAME pillars, 118–119
    value, 84–85
SWOT (strengths, weaknesses,
        opportunities, and threats),
        9, 22–25, 101
    exercise, 25
    objectives of, 23
    opportunities, 24
    strengths, 23
    threats, 24
    weaknesses, 24

Take Away, 147
Talent, leadership, and culture
    giving teams a voice, 210–211
    beyond one workforce, 208
    power of involvement, 209–210
    processes create clarity, bureaucracy
        kills energy, 209
    turning point of change, 211–212
Technology
    digital commerce, 155–162
    Digital Services Economy,
        141–145
    generative AI, strategic impacts of,
        162–167
    globalization, digital shortcut to,
        151–154
        Mrs. Sarah's Shop, 152–153
    hypothesis-driven strategy,
        170–178
        Mrs. Sarah's Shop, 176
    models that support decision
        making, 178–185

Fresh Paintings, 180–181
silent disruption and digital twins,
        145–151
    digital twin approach, 150–151
    ladder of sophistication,
        146–149
    strategic role, 103–104
    ten tips for getting technology
        right, 167–170
Telemedicine, 191
Tesla, 126
Think Digital, Beyond Digital, 221
TikTok, 160, 162
Tracking, SCRIPT framework, 194
Transform, set the foundations to
    business strategy, 116–122
        Shifting to a Subscription
        Model, 120–121
    vision first, 108–115
        Lightening Furniture, 114
        Real Time Cleaning, 112–114
Transformation Modeling Canvas,
        178, 182–183
Travel agency, 47–49
Trivago, 154
Trust Theory, 204
Twitter, 80–81, 85
Tynan, Caroline, 66

Uber, 16, 42, 48, 72, 73, 76, 77, 104
Uber Eats, 18, 29, 51, 147
Uber Freight, 42

Value chain, 85–100, 153
Value, customer, 74–85

Walmart, 155
Warehouse management system
        (WMS), 114, 192
WhatsApp, 73
Windows/Office, 142

XaaS, 142

YouTube, 160, 162

Zalando, 160
Zhang, Daniel, 156

www.ingramcontent.com/pod-product-compliance
Lightning Source LLC
Chambersburg PA
CBHW061504180526
45171CB00001B/33